Eight Plays from Off-Off Broadway

Eight Plays from Off-Off Broadway

Edited by
Nick Orzel and Michael Smith

With an Introduction
by Michael Smith

THE BOBBS-MERRILL COMPANY, INC.
A Subsidiary of HOWARD W. SAMS & CO., INC.
PUBLISHERS/INDIANAPOLIS · NEW YORK · KANSAS CITY

Contents

Eight Plays from Off-Off Broadway

Introduction

The relationship between Off-Off Broadway theatre and the new playwrights is symbiotic. They invented it because they were unwanted elsewhere; it invented them because it needed new plays. Neither would exist without the other.

That is the subject of this book: Off-Off Broadway and the new playwrights. Once reasoned into existence, the subject splits into two. The playwrights are doing what young playwrights always do—getting their plays performed wherever they can. Off-Off Broadway is a place for them to learn; it gives them incentive as well as experience. For the playwrights it is a step toward normalcy, the healthiest development in years.

But Off-Off Broadway turns out to be a novel form of theatre, not just a training ground. It is amateur theatre done largely by professionals. It is theatre with no resources but the most sophisticated audience in America. It is both casual community theatre and dedicated experimental theatre. It is proposing an alternative to an established theatre which hardly knows it exists. It may be that the playwrights are less revolutionary than their context.

Remove the playwrights, though, and Off-Off Broadway has no identity. It consists of coffeehouses and churches and workshops and organizers and angels that stage noncommercial productions of new plays in New York that won't fit into any other category. They all have different ideas about what they're doing, different standards, different goals, different kinds of places to do it in. Practically everyone knows practically everyone else, but a social scene doesn't make an art movement. There is no manifesto, no

1

social or aesthetic program, no shared mystique. No place is definitive or even typical of Off-Off Broadway. Maybe there's no such thing. But it is also commonly said that there are no new American playwrights.

Read this book. Here are eight new American playwrights, and their plays are very good. Off-Off Broadway has produced them and dozens more, hundreds more, and it looks like the fun's just starting.

My feelings about Off-Off Broadway are complicated and personal. I was on hand for its birth and have seen its growing pains; I feel like a fond uncle. I have reviewed its productions for years in *The Village Voice*; I feel like a proud parole officer. I have spent nights till dawn setting up lights for its productions and felt like a patient servant. I have directed two plays and been exhilarated by idealism, freedom, and indifference to the terrors of cultural commerce. It has given two of my plays their first and only productions; I know its value and rewards for beginning playwrights. It's a place to go even when I'm sick of theatre. It's a place to do real work when I'm turning too much into a critic. It's a place to see my friends. I feel like a member of the club.

Off-Off Broadway is decidedly clubby. To some extent it has a coterie audience; to some extent it is snobbish and self-glorifying; to some extent it is a playground. Sometimes it is despicable. But all these weaknesses are inseparable from its strength, which is its human scale. The established theatre has fallen into the hands of professionals, and they have fallen into the attitude of detachment. The distinction between the practice of an art and the performance of a job or assigned task is lost. Off-Off Broadway there is neither pay nor negotiable publicity, and thus no way to evade the personal commitment of every choice.

There are few occasions for personal commitment in the commercial theatre today. The structure is industrial—the "entertainment industry"—and the product tends to be generalized, fixed, packaged diversion, coldly performed and passively to be watched; like television and the movies, it is indifferent to the spectator. In Broadway theatres I sometimes imagine that the proscenium is filled in with glass, that the stage is really a huge television screen, that the actors are not really there. And often they're not: they are just "doing a job." Seeing the theatre in these terms— to permit it to become this—denies its nature, which is to join performers and spectators in a mutual experience. Off-Off Broadway can make this process palpable.

When I began reviewing plays for the *Voice* eight years ago, there was no such thing as Off-Off Broadway. Plain Off-Broadway was young and healthy and seemed to have endless possibilities. Off-Broadway was a place to do work which was impracticable under the hit-or-flop rules of Broadway but needed to be done anyway. This consisted chiefly of the modern masters, including Genet, Brecht, Beckett, Pirandello, even Ibsen and Chekhov, who had everything but box-office appeal; and the serious new play-wrights. The last playwrights of stature to emerge via Broadway had been Tennessee Williams and Arthur Miller, in the forties. By the late fifties young writers had mostly given up on the theatre—why write for the stage if there is no stage available?

Off-Broadway opened things up for several good years. A handful of productions won great popularity—most notably three musicals, *The Threepenny Opera, Little Mary Sunshine,* and *The Fantasticks* (which is running forever). In addition, Off-Broadway gave productions, often excellent, to countless plays old and new which would not other-

wise have been seen and without which the American theatre would be poorer, its audiences even more dispirited
and depleted. It enabled young actors and other theatre
artists to gain experience, which had become nearly impossible in this country, and to work on plays from which they
could learn.

Off-Broadway's outstanding playwright was Edward Albee, whose *The Zoo Story* opened in 1960 on a bill with
Beckett's *Krapp's Last Tape*. Albee had two more plays
done off Broadway—*The American Dream* and *The Death
of Bessie Smith*—before moving uptown with *Who's Afraid
of Virginia Woolf?* The one other playwright who moved
from Off-Broadway *(The Typists* and *The Tiger)* to Broadway success *(Luv)* was Murray Schisgal. But pairing Albee
and Schisgal reveals nothing but the lack of coherent
values: the serious playwright has no reliable guide to
choosing a goal for himself and no way of measuring his
progress toward it. Novelty rules, and achievement wins
only momentary respect; because of two bad plays in a row,
for example, Tennessee Williams has now been abandoned
by audiences and pronounced finished by critics.

Off-Broadway introduced a large number of new playwrights in its golden years, and their present obscurity is
obviously no measure of merit. They include Jack Richard-
son *(The Prodigal)*, Jack Gelber *(The Connection)*, William Hanley *(Mrs. Dally Has a Lover)*, Arthur Kopit *(Oh
Dad, Poor Dad, Mamma's Hung You in the Closet and I'm
Feelin' So Sad)*, William Snyder *(The Days and Nights of
Beebee Fenstermaker)*, Kenneth H. Brown *(The Brig)*, and
Adrienne Kennedy *(Funnyhouse of a Negro)*.

But Off-Broadway's happy days were over quicker than
anyone expected; ironically nearly a dozen new Off-
Broadway theatres were built or reconstructed just too late,
and Off-Broadway today is glutted with empty theatres. As

the movement became established, rents went up, unions moved in, ticket prices climbed, audiences were reduced in number and ever more subject to "hit psychology." A play could be produced for a few hundred dollars in the middle fifties; in the sixties Off-Broadway productions have required initial investments ranging from a minimum of almost $10,000 to upwards of $40,000. To risk putting on an untried or unconventional play became foolhardy, at least without plenty of money and high-powered publicity. The pressure to play it commercially safe has steadily mounted and the opportunities for creative work have steadily diminished. The Living Theatre, which for several years had been Off-Broadway's most adventurous theatre, was closed for nonpayment of taxes in October 1963. Since that time, with a few exceptions, Off-Broadway has been in decline.

Out of this history Off-Off Broadway has been created. Most of its efforts are devoted to new plays, and another whole group of playwrights—much larger—has appeared. The designation "Off-Off Broadway" is cumbersome and misleading, since it suggests that Off-Off Broadway has the same relation to Off-Broadway that Off-Broadway has to Broadway; but it gives a nice sense of the obscurity of the "movement."

Off-Off Broadway started, actually, as a way-station on the road to success. But disenchantment with conventional definitions of success is now widespread, and Off-Off Broadway increasingly is seen as an alternative to the established theatre rather than a way into it. Increasingly those who work Off-Off Broadway have learned to value the freedom it offers and discovered that work done there can be more rewarding despite its smaller scale, and sometimes superior in quality; and they have begun to relinquish their traditional dreams. It is a difficult choice. It means giving up the reassurance of public acceptance. It means financial hardship as well, since Off-Off Broadway operates virtually without funds, its productions often paid for by the artists themselves. Several of the Off-Off Broadway playwrights represented in this book—Lanford Wilson, Jean-Claude van Itallie, Sam Shepard, Paul Foster—have also had commercial Off-Broadway productions; the experience has almost always been painful and disappointing to them. Off-Off Broadway is viable artistically—despite physical inadequacies, in-group audiences, and limited runs. Financially it is in urgent need of a new idea, and none is in sight.

Off-Off Broadway's birthday can be given, somewhat arbitrarily, as September 27, 1960. On that date a production of Alfred Jarry's *King Ubu* opened at a Greenwich Village coffeehouse called the Take 3. The program contained an inspirational note: "This production . . . represents a return to the original idea of Off-Broadway theatre, in which imagination is substituted for money, and plays can be presented in a way that would be impossible in the commercial theatre." A few weeks later the term "Off-Off Broadway" was coined in print by Jerry Tallmer, then theatre critic of *The Village Voice*.

Off-Off Broadway has gone through many changes in the past six years, most of them dictated by various agencies of the City of New York. Following *Ubu* came a flood of cafe-theatre productions, erratically organized and ragged in quality. Before long the City reminded the cafes that they were not licensed for such activities; in fact no such licenses were possible. (The Caffe Cino, which actually antedates *Ubu,* in an interminable series of narrow squeaks managed to evade this edict. It is the only survivor from those pioneer days.) When the License Department couldn't do the job, the Fire and Buildings Departments would inspect the premises and discover costly violations.

Civic hostility to Off-Off Broadway periodically rose to mysterious, weirdly vindictive heights. The cafes gave up drama, in any event, and Off-Off Broadway almost disappeared.

But the seeds were germinating. Off-Broadway theatres are normally dark on Monday nights, and before long Monday was the busiest night in the week. The Living Theatre diversified itself and its audience by sponsoring a series of Monday events of all kinds—poetry readings, filmstage, concerts of music and dance, and everything else. Judson Memorial Church on Washington Square permitted a congregation member who had written a play to stage it in the choir loft; this led to the formation of the Judson Poets' Theatre in 1961. The Hardware Poets' Playhouse ran intermittently for several years in a loft upstairs from a midtown hardware store. Ellen Stewart founded her Cafe La Mama in frank emulation of the Caffe Cino; she qualifies as most-persecuted of Off-Off Broadway's impresarios, having been hounded out of three locations in turn. Edward Albee and his producers supported a Playwrights' Unit, giving workshop performances of new writers' plays for invited audiences; LeRoi Jones's *Dutchman* moved from there to Off-Broadway acclaim. At St. Mark's Church in-the-Bouwerie on the Lower East Side (which has replaced Greenwich Village as New York's low-rent artists' district) Theatre Genesis was founded in 1964. Unlike the others, the American Theatre for Poets concentrated on plays by poets; it had several short seasons in various locations and persuaded fine artists to make sets. Always the off-and-on Monday nights continued, all over town, sometimes pointless, sometimes extraordinary; Frank O'Hara's *The General Returns from One Place to Another* was one of them.

All these efforts were devoted to new plays by new playwrights. Within two or three years the demand for new plays had zoomed from almost zero to ten or fifteen a month. (The two cafes, Cino and La Mama, were each producing a different play every week.)

At first there were too few new plays—one saw as well early Tennessee Williams one-acts, acting-class adaptations of short stories, fragments of all kinds; but also Beckett's radio plays *All That Fall* and *Embers*, pirated but memorable. And at first the good productions were exceptions; good actors and directors, still sanguine about the commercial theatre, were reluctant to work under these makeshift, no-pay conditions.

Gradually demand created supply. Word got around that new plays were wanted, and new playwrights appeared bearing scripts. Most of them were no good, but in those days they were put on anyway, and the writers either learned or got discouraged and went away. Off-Off Broadway has always been permissive; even today, with scripts pouring in and directors begging for dates, selectivity is erratic and quality totally unpredictable.

This is a moment of rare stability. It is possible right now to say where Off-Off Broadway is, if not what it is. Four places—one cafe, one theatre club, two churches—provide space and sponsorship for most of the current projects; a group called the Open Theatre gives productions of its own and unites many of the actors, directors, and playwrights who work everywhere else. This book is accordingly divided into five sections, the plays grouped according to who presented them. Independent productions still come and go; Frank O'Hara's play was one and is placed independently at the beginning of this book.

The Caffe Cino occupies a smallish "storefront" on a slightly hard-to-find street in the middle of Greenwich Vil-

lage. It opened in 1958 and soon found itself doing plays.
It is the only true cafe-theatre now functioning in New
York and offers an elaborate menu of food and nonalco-
holic drinks in addition to twice-nightly performances of
plays (three times on Fridays and Saturdays). It is a narrow
room, crowded with tables and chairs, its walls bedecked
with an astonishing array of frivolous and extravagant
decorations. Most plays there are less than an hour long
and are done on platforms halfway along one wall, with
the audience ranged about them on three sides; sometimes various parts of the room are used, sometimes the
whole room, and occasionally a proscenium has even been
set up at one end. Theatricality at the Cino depends greatly
on its excellent lighting setup. The audience, eating and
drinking at the tables, is inches from the actors, and the
cluttered coziness of the room unites performers and spectators into a single event. Ordinarily the program at the Cino
changes every week, but Lanford Wilson's *The Madness of
Lady Bright* broke the pattern. It was the most successful
production in the cafe's history and, in three separate productions, ran for a total of sixteen weeks.

Judson Memorial Church is a handsome Italianate building on the south side of Washington Square. Inside, its
main room is spacious and serene, dominated at one end
by a huge, simple wooden cross, at the other by a large choir
loft. Most of the Judson Poets' Theatre productions have
been performed in the choir loft. Judson presents seven or
eight theatre programs a year, usually consisting of two
one-act plays and running for three or four weekends. The
theatre is one arm of an arts project which includes a gallery and the important Judson Dance Theatre; Judson also
sponsored several of the earliest "happenings." The entire
arts project is run by Al Carmines, Judson's young and
progressive assistant minister, who pursues the church's

purposes through a policy of noninterference. Carmines is also an extraordinarily talented theatre composer who has written scores for many Judson productions, including plays by Gertrude Stein, Maria Irene Fornes, Rosalyn Drexler, George Dennison, Ruth Krauss, and H. M. Koutoukas. Outstanding work at Judson has also been done by two directors, Lawrence Kornfeld (formerly of the Living Theatre) and Remy Charlip (formerly of the children's Paper Bag Players). Judson has, on the whole, produced the best work yet seen Off-Off Broadway and has built up a loyal and enthusiastic audience. Its performances are free and usually packed.

La Mama Experimental Theatre Club hides out in a large second-story loft on Second Avenue, once the Broadway of the Yiddish-language theatre. La Mama avoids bureaucratic harassment only by maintaining secrecy—its address and phone number are never advertised—and people miss plays at La Mama because they can't find it. Even so, most nights the house is full; performances are Wednesday through Sunday, usually for one week per play. La Mama is a modified cafe: its spectator-members sit at small tables, pay one dollar a week dues, and are offered a choice of instant coffee, instant tea, or instant hot chocolate. La Mama has a permanent raised stage with curtain at one end of the room, but plays have been given in arena style, with half the audience up on the stage. Ellen Stewart, La Mama herself, supports the theatre by designing bathing suits. She does no actual theatre work but is limitlessly devoted to "her" playwrights: she sent companies of actors to Paris and Copenhagen to perform the plays, a Cafe La Mama has opened in Bogota, Colombia, she has masterminded Off-Broadway productions, and her faith in the work being done is infectious and inexhaustible.

10

Theatre Genesis is the youngest and most modest of Off-Off Broadway's big four. Sponsored by the arts program of St. Mark's Church in-the-Bouwerie, it is much more consciously purposive than Judson's theatre. The St. Mark's community has changed radically: what was once a fashionable Episcopalian parish is now a near-slum. The dynamic minister of St. Mark's, Michael Allen, established the arts program to help reopen communications between church and community. Ralph Cook, lay minister to the arts at St. Mark's, runs the program and Theatre Genesis. His allegiance, like Ellen Stewart's, is to the playwrights; he further believes that the work of the theatre must have relevance to the life and spirit of the community. He runs a weekly playwrights' workshop, with actors present strictly to serve the playwrights. Productions are given, usually for three weekends, whenever he finds plays he likes. They are performed in a fair-sized, squarish room upstairs in the Paris Hall, a space lacking theatricality but sufficiently neutral to suit many of the plays Cook chooses. Cook is himself a director but is trying to develop a group of directors, actors, and playwrights who can work together consistently in a community spirit. Theatre Genesis opened in 1964 with *Cowboys* and *The Rock Garden,* by the previously unknown and unproduced Sam Shepard; the discovery of Shepard is its major achievement to date.

The Open Theatre is a group of actors, directors, playwrights, designers, musicians, and critics who meet in workshop sessions for various purposes. They have spent several years developing an acting ensemble, and regularly sponsor productions. The first performances were demonstrations of workshop projects and mostly improvisational; the group has steadily moved toward the production of plays, by its member playwrights and others. After several Monday-night series, during the 1965–66 season the Open Theatre allied itself with La Mama, where it gave one play a month. The Open Theatre's importance in Off-Off Broadway is its penetration, the fact that its membership includes many of the most active playwrights, directors, and actors. (This book includes plays by four of its members—Jean-Claude van Itallie, Megan Terry, Maria Irene Fornes, and Sam Shepard.) Some of the playwrights have worked closely with the acting workshops (especially van Itallie and Terry), and the actors have worked together continuously to create a technique for the new plays, many of which are difficult or impossible to perform with conventional acting methods.

Although no stylistic bias guided our selection of plays for this anthology, it turns out that none is naturalistic. Instead they are anti-illusionistic: the spectator is constantly being reminded that he is watching a theatrical event, not a representation of outside reality. This effect is characteristic of the entire modern theatre, not only of Off-Off Broadway, and it is interesting to note the variety of techniques by which it is accomplished.

None of the plays is a conventional comedy (Fornes and O'Hara are ironic in their use of vaudeville and revue traditions) but virtually all are comic, at least in part. This too is characteristic of Off-Off Broadway and of the generation to which these writers belong. Irony, indirection, and self-mockery are dominant tones, suggesting that it would be dangerous or indiscreet or "uncool" to speak more openly. Ironic tone and anti-naturalistic technique both give the writer some detachment from his subject; the plays' theatricality becomes a shield, sometimes against sentimentality (narrowly avoided in the Wilson play), sometimes against direct involvement. None of the plays except Wilson's makes open or specific comment about the actual experiences and emotions of contemporary life; they are, on the whole, theatrical rather than dramatic. It is interesting to note, too, that none of the plays expresses a political commitment. (*America Hurrah* is a strong but general attack on popular values.) But all the plays (except one, *Balls*) are strikingly American and modern in style, frame of reference, and sensibility: they could not have been written anywhere else or at any other time.

The plays speak more than adequately for themselves—especially from the stage—and I hope this book will lead to productions. I want to discuss them briefly only to indicate effects they had in performance that may not be evident from reading the scripts; and to mention certain techniques that are original to these playwrights.

Paul Foster's *Balls* is the most eccentric of the plays. Its text is beautifully written and, surprisingly, sounds Irish, reminiscent of Beckett and Synge. Its subject matter has a strange, total lack of immediacy; its images are literary, evoking associations to literary experience rather than real life; its presentational method creates disorientation. Seeing the play, I was held in tension between the calm of detachment and the disquiet of mysteriousness. The play's auditory content, recorded on tape, sounded perfectly realistic although obviously fantasy; nothing was visible on stage except two white ping-pong balls swinging steadily and meaninglessly in a void. The play's strength lies in its contradictions, I think, particularly in the disjunctions between realism and abstraction, between rational and arbitrary levels of action.

Megan Terry's *Calm Down Mother* is a "transformation play." This is a new technique, derived directly from the Open Theatre's workshop experiments. The Open Theatre was seeking ways to do theatre without relying on money; the "transformation" work, continuing experiments created by Viola Spolin in Chicago, in effect substituted acting devices for sets, costumes, lighting effects, or large casts. *Calm Down Mother* was one of the first plays using this technique, which greatly increased the range of action available to the playwright and enabled her to move freely around in her subject. The play uses transformation of both character and place; on a bare stage the three actresses move through a variety of roles and locales without any logical transitions. Transformations make exceptional—and welcome—demands on the audience's imagination.

Frank O'Hara was primarily a poet rather than a playwright. This is evident in his play, which is distinguished for the clarity, precision, and economy of its language and the delicate, tender whimsy of its wit. The play is satirical but extraordinarily cool and gentle. Taylor Mead, a brilliantly eccentric comic actor, played the General and achieved an amazing double-image of hilarity and lyrical sweetness.

Sam Shepard's *Chicago* seems to me the most original of the plays. Shepard is a highly visual playwright, both in the stage pictures he contrives and in the words his characters speak. He discards the standard ingredients of drama: the action of *Chicago* is barely coherent and relatively trivial, its characters are no more than outlines. Instead Shepard uses images in an almost unitary way, lining them up in disjointed associative sequence, crowding them brusquely into the spectator's mind. *Chicago* may be difficult to read, since it confounds rational analysis and relies on immediate visual impact. In performance it is both funny and touching and builds up considerable momentum. Without knowing anything very specific about its main character, one feels strongly the precise shape and density of his desperation, sharing it enough to find the coda of breathing a great release.

Jean-Claude van Itallie's doll-play *America Hurrah* is a nightmare vision of contemporary America. Welding form and content, the play is bloated, coarse, a juggernaut of vulgarity. Van Itallie tries to shock the audience in order to convey his own sense of shock; in becoming as revolting as its subject, the play is enormously forceful.

Maria Irene Fornes makes a related point in a diametrically opposite style in her bouncy vaudeville *The Successful Life of 3*. Its characters are brightly cold-blooded, ingratiating monsters, and in performance the play is chilling because so very charming.

Joel Oppenheimer's *The Great American Desert* is a nostalgic look into the American past, its romanticism controlled by objectivity in language and form. The matter-of-fact heroism and individualism of its characters comments clearly if indirectly on the American present. Oppenheimer is a poet who avoids sounding "poetic," and I find his play to be enormously likable.

Lanford Wilson's *The Madness of Lady Bright* is an anti-tragedy with a very contemporary anti-hero: an aging homosexual. Leslie Bright has returned society's insults by adopting outrageous mannerisms; in his behavior he reverses emotions as well as sexes: loneliness becomes disdain, desperation humor. His honesty, though, is unmistakably brave. By making us laugh with him and at him, he becomes heroic despite the distorted style; but self-mockery is too brittle a defense against despair, and the play describes his disintegration. As a psycho-sociological document the play is appalling; as drama it is tremendously poignant.

The diversity of these plays only suggests Off-Off Broadway's achievement. Many more plays would be needed to map its range; we were sorry not to be able to include plays by Rosalyn Drexler, H. M. Koutoukas, Diane di Prima,

Leonard Melfi, George Dennison, David Starkweather, Rochelle Owens, LeRoi Jones, Ronald Tavel, Robert Nichols—to name only a few. There will be more plays and more books and more playwrights—and more theatre movements. Off-Off Broadway is a promise.

MICHAEL SMITH

16

The General Returns from One Place to Another

THE GENERAL RETURNS FROM ONE PLACE TO ANOTHER
was first produced by Present Stages at the Writer's Stage Theatre on
March 23, 1964. It was directed by Jerry Benjamin with the following cast:

THE GENERAL	Taylor Mead
AIDE #1 (BERT)	John Worden
AIDE #2 (EDGAR)	Jeffrey Reiss
MRS. FORBES	Veronica Castang
GENERALISSIMO CHIANG KAI-SHEK	Loren Bivens
GENERALISSIMO FRANCO	James Spruill
CONSTANCE (LUOA)	Yvette Hawkins
MME. CHIANG KAI-SHEK	Mari-Claire Charba
TIE SALESMAN	Glyn Turman
NATIVES AND CITIZENS	Joanne Hargarther, Susan Shawn, Jacque Lynn Colton, Mark Duffy, Marilyn Lee, Darnell Beatty, Bernard Johnson

FRANK O'HARA *was born in Baltimore, Maryland, in 1926, and
died in July 1966. He attended Harvard University (B.A. 1950) and
the University of Michigan (M.A. 1951), where he received the Hop-
wood Award in Poetry. He had published six books of poems:* A City
Winter, Meditations in an Emergency, Second Avenue, Odes, Lunch
Poems *and* Love Poems *(tentative title). He was the author of five one-
act plays:* Love's Labor, Try Try, Awake in Spain, The General Returns from One Place to Another, *and* What Century? *He was the author of* Jackson Pollock, *a monograph published by Braziller. From
1951 to 1966 he worked at the Museum of Modern Art, where he organized and prepared catalogues for exhibitions of New Spanish
Painting and Sculpture, Franz Kline, Robert Motherwell, Reuben
Nakian, and David Smith.*

The General Returns from One Place to Another

by Frank O'Hara

To Vincent Warren and to Warner Brothers and Taylor Mead

SCENE 1

(Scurvy, an island community famous in the last century largely for the betel nut craze of its inhabitants, which led to cannibalism. They stand in a small group center, waving small paper replicas of the flag of their country, which is solid black. The GENERAL enters almost nude but wearing galoshes and a topee. For each scene thereafter, the GENERAL will enter with one more article of clothing added, decorations, etc.)

GENERAL
(Saluting cheerfully)
I'm on my way BACK!

NATIVES
(Impassively)
Hooray.
(GENERAL crosses and exits discouraged.)

SCENE 2

(A camp in the jungle. Two aides lounging about, rather sloppily dressed. Enter GENERAL, crosses to card table and examines some correspondence.)

21

GENERAL
(Musing)
There's something very wrong with the state of things . . .
people's attitudes . . . . Something very wrong indeed.

1ST AIDE
I'll say there is. I don't know what's gotten into people.
And there isn't even a war on. It beats me.

2ND AIDE
And nobody pays any attention to us. Here we are taking
this long arduous trip, and not so much as a reporter has
shown up for three weeks!

GENERAL
Well, I know it.
(Turning)
And what about yourselves? You might at least come to at-
tention or something.

AIDES
(Together)
We don't have to, we're out of uniform, aren't we?

GENERAL
Oh never mind. Just get me a banana, one of you.

SCENE 3
*(An inn on the outskirts. The GENERAL is standing at the bar
drinking, somewhat as if he were waiting for Sadie Thomp-
son. He is not at all drunk.)*

GENERAL
Well, my good man?

BARTENDER
Okay.
(Starts fixing another whiskey and soda.)

GENERAL

Bit brisk, the weather, for these parts, isn't it?

BARTENDER

It's practically a cold wave, it must be down to 92 or 93 degrees.

GENERAL

Yes, it makes a man feel vigorous when the temperature goes down.

BARTENDER

If it goes down.

GENERAL

Of course. Certainly it must go down first, that is *if* a man's going to feel vigorous.

BARTENDER

Exactly.

GENERAL

Hmmmm.
   (A lady in organdy enters, with parasol and picture hat.)

BARTENDER

Good afternoon, Mrs. Forbes. How are you feeling today?

MRS. FORBES

Divine! It's this magnificent chill that's come upon us so suddenly.

BARTENDER

Yes indeed. What'll it be?

MRS. FORBES

A pink gin, I think, though it is early in the day for one.

GENERAL
   (Amiably)
It's never *too* early in the day.

MRS. FORBES

I beg your pardon. I wish you soldiers had never discovered
these islands.

GENERAL
(Drawing himself up)
I wish you ladies had never discovered drink!

1ST AIDE
(In doorway)
General, the jeep is ready.
(Looking in)
Hey, who's the chick? Is she coming too?

GENERAL

Shut up, you fool!
(To BARTENDER)
I seem to be a little short . . .

BARTENDER

That's okay, General, it's on the island.
(They shake hands)

GENERAL
(Exiting)
Thank you. It's a fine establishment you have here.

MRS. FORBES
(Calling after him as he exits)
You brute!
(To BARTENDER)
Who was that anyway?

BARTENDER

I don't know. From his conversation he must be some kind
of . . . intellectual, I guess.

MRS. FORBES

Oh . . . They don't last long out here, those sort of people.

24

SCENE 4

(Outside the Opera House in Saigon, late afternoon, only a very few people about. A TIE SALESMAN *enters with a little rack of ties held aloft.)*

TIE SALESMAN

Little did I think I'd ever sell a *tie* to a General! Especially as I never have any army regulation ties to sell because I'm afraid of being accused of theft or Black Marketry. Nevertheless he bought one of my finest just-before-sundown colored ties and put it on on the spot. His aides were stupefied!

1ST CITIZEN

What did he look like, this General?

TIE SALESMAN

He was a big, grand-looking man. Looked as if he fitted his rank, or station I believe they say in the Occident. Had lived in Paris for six months once. *That* part was very interesting. He's out to explain why he's coming back. But the odd thing, the Chief of the Radio Station, who is another customer of mine, says he doesn't know who he is. I thought they might want to interview him, but no soap. Oh, that's another funny thing about it all. By the merest luck, I happened to have a tube of toothpaste on me, and he bought it for FIVE NEW FRANCS, which as you may know is 500 old ones. How's that for good fortune?

ALL CITIZENS ON STAGE

MAGNIFICENT!

SCENE 5

(The observation platform [rear] of a train chugging through a pass. Seated on it smoking cigars with their feet up on the

25

railing [they're in canvas chairs] are AIDES *1 & 2, hereafter called* BERT *and* EDGAR. *They are more or less in uniform, but each has on a very loud tie.)*

EDGAR

Terrific scenery, Bert. I hope old Smokey stays asleep so we can enjoy it for a while.

BERT

I don't know whether it's worse worrying about him asleep or awake. I think he's flipping his lid, Edgar, honest I do.

EDGAR

I don't think it's as serious as all that, Bert. He's always been peculiar. But I'm getting pretty tired of sending all those cables for permission to visit Chungking. What's he want to go to Chungking for?

BERT

He doesn't. It's a nervous tic. He only wants to go to places he's already been.

(MRS. FORBES *enters.*)

MRS. FORBES

I beg your pardon. I didn't know the platform was occupied. Do you suppose there'd be room for me to get a glimpse of this magnificent view before night closes in?

EDGAR

Say! Didn't I meet you in that bar in Borneo a couple of weeks ago? You were wearing a big flimsy hat?

MRS. FORBES

Why yes, young man, I thought you looked familiar! I think I'd like some gin.

EDGAR
(*Leaping up*)

Yes, ma'am! Right away.
(Exits)

BERT

My name is . . .

MRS. FORBES

Oh never mind. We travelers seldom remember names, hardly even faces. I find that I remember forms more readily. You know, temples, natives, that sort of thing. Isn't the landscape of Nepal astounding?

BERT

We were here before with the old man. It's nicer this time, though.

MRS. FORBES

The old man?

BERT

Uh . . . our employer.

MRS. FORBES

Poor boys! It's so terrible to work, when there's so much in the world to see, to enjoy!

BERT

Yes, ma'am.

SCENE 6

(Singapore Airport. The GENERAL is out on the field with two technicians taping an interview for the "Voice of America." He's wearing his tie, too. Behind them, a big airplane. The GENERAL carries a spray of orchids.)

GENERAL

I'll tell you one thing, boys, the welcome . . . Are we shooting? I mean, are we getting it down?

1st TECHNICIAN

Not yet, sir.

2nd TECHNICIAN

Now sir! Now she's taking!

GENERAL

I'll tell you one thing, boys, the welcome, it's been magnificent here in ol' Sing. I mean half the world is asleep, a *good* half if my experience is any measure, and I can assure you I haven't been conked out at the switch. But here in Singapore the sun is shining and they know who I am and they know I'm back. Well, I came back for that—so they'd know it. Know what this is? It's a spray of orchids given to yours truly by the sweetest little Eurasian girl you ever saw. That's respect for you—thought I was the Viceroy of India, as if India had a Viceroy any more. (It doesn't, does it?—better check that inch with Central Int.)

Anyhow, I'm not vain. The point is to come back, not to be recognized. Art's long, and conquered people are short. That's why they don't recognize me: THEY DON'T EVEN SEE ME!

But this experience, like (and I feel I can say this honestly and with full conviction—ugly word, that, conviction) . . . like all experiences, has been a wonderful one. It's given me a lot, and I think I've grown a lot from experiencing the particular experience I've been experiencing. It's a matter, I decided the other day in a rather drafty club car on the way from Djakarta, it's all a matter of handling. Let me give you a very simple illustration of what I mean that everybody all over the world will get. Will understand.

We all know that it takes handling, *handling*, to get anything done, to get anywhere. Now let's take a simple example. Does anyone actually believe that if Marion Davies had been properly handled she wouldn't have been a bigger star than Norma Shearer? That's what I mean by handling. Handling is taking a poetic, no I'll go further, an *optimistic*, view of reality—AND MAKING IT STICK. That girl had everything (Marion)—big blue eyes, a gorgeous chassis, a voice—good God, she made a movie with Bing Crosby, didn't she? And what did Norma have? Well, she was a good enough actress, even a pretty one: but she had a wall-eye. What happened, you'll ask, and I'll tell you, I've thought this out, I'm not like some Senator on the floor playing with his blocks: what happened is MISMANAGE-MENT, or THE HANDLING WAS WRONG.

Now this problem is the most important one of our time and should be taken up with the U.N. It's at the root of what in the thirties used to be called "All Evil." Well, these are better times, but not *much* better, and the free peoples of the world had better take all of this into account when deciding the fate of all the free and unfree peoples of the world. I'm not going to go into the career of Louis B. Mayer in the latter connection right now, it's too upsetting.

Anyway, thanks boys, and wish me a happy voyage.

TECHNICIANS
(Together)
Gee, that was wonderful. Have a terrific climb, General.

GENERAL
Onwards and backwards, boys!
(Salutes and exits into plane.)

SCENE 7

(A fashionable hat shop run by a Chinese woman. MRS. FORBES *is trying on hats.)*

MRS. FORBES

It's so sweet of those poor boys to do this for me! I think I'll take this one with all the feathers. I never go any place, so they couldn't possibly get crushed.

CHINESE WOMAN

You are very wise, White Lady.

SCENE 8

(GENERALISSIMI CHIANG KAI-SHEK *and* FRANCO *seated in camp chairs outside a pup tent in the Spanish hills. Early morning; they are drinking coffee served by two orderlies.*)

CHIANG

I'm telling you he's becoming the scourge of the South Pacific! He's always nosing about, poking his way into other people's affairs, mumbling something sad about what it's like to "return." Well, who asked him to return?

FRANCO

I guess that cover of *Newsweek* went to his head. But cheer up, things are bad all over. We all have our troubles. Europe's no bed of roses.

CHIANG

Well it's no bed of saffron, either. How would you like it if the Commies had control of Gibraltar?

FRANCO

We'd rout them out, by God, that's what we'd do.

CHIANG

Well don't look now, but . . .

SCENE 9

(*The office of a Travel Agent.* MRS. FORBES, *again in organdy but wearing her feathered hat this time, is being waited on*

by a CLERK *while a* GOVERNMENT AGENT *in a Malayan turban
stands by, curious but impassive.)*

CLERK

Perhaps these pamphlets will help you to decide, Mrs. . . .
It was Mrs. Forbes, I believe?

MRS. FORBES

Oh I've decided already, I've made up my mind. I want to
go to Spain. I want to go to India first. I think I'd adore
Hyderabad. Then by a very slow freighter or something
through the Indian Ocean, rounding I should hope that
corner where that curious little place is, you know: Aden!
Then through the Suez Canal, if they've got it working
properly, and on by Tripoli, and Carthage, and the Kasbah
—oh! it's so romantic, I don't know how I'll ever pay for
it all! And then there I'll be, I'll hop off Gibraltar like a
goat and land in SPAIN!

CLERK

That is a delightful plan. Let me just go and check the
route and accommodations for you.
(Exits)

GOVERNMENT AGENT

Now that I know you are definitely planning to leave our
country, I am able to tell you that you will not be allowed
to leave our country. That is our way here. We never cause
anyone any anxiety until they force us to. You could have
gone on living peacefully here without ever knowing, but
it is not our fault that you brought this unfortunate cir-
cumstance about. Your papers are not in order. That's why
I've been shadowing you all through the streets and byways
of our glorious city for these several weeks, to see what
you're up to.

MRS. FORBES

Well I must say that's flattering! You must have so many

other things to do! . . . And as for the trip, not taking it will be better for my hat.

SCENE 10

(The GENERAL *walking about an extinguished campfire. Early morning. A pup tent in the rear with four feet sticking out of it.)*

GENERAL

Morning. Morning, and they haven't polished my shoes and they haven't gotten up and they haven't started the fire and they haven't made the coffee yet. The funny thing is that they're both broke from buying that strange woman all those presents. How dare they act this way to me?—not that I'm in any position to fire them. The lower orders have strange habits of independence, especially when in the direst of straits.

I think continually of the Naga tribesmen. What a strange and desperate desire is theirs.

To be independent—how ironic and how lovely! As if anyone could be! And if one were, immediately the others would arrive and tear you down, exploit you, rape you, and murder you. "Self-determination!" What an odd slogan. One might as well have a slogan reading: "Impossible!"

(Shaking off the mood and growing furious)

WAKE UP, YOU IRRESPONSIBLE . . . !

SCENE 11

(Same scene. The two AIDES *are finishing preparing coffee over the campfire and* BERT *hands the* GENERAL *his cup.)*

BERT

Here you are, General. It sure takes a long time to make coffee in the tropics.

GENERAL

It takes a long time to wake up, too.

EDGAR

(Cheerfully)

It sure does, doesn't it?

GENERAL

I didn't mean that as a compliment.

BERT

It's been my experience of life that the most important people always wake up early.

EDGAR

That's been my experience of life, too.

GENERAL

(Flattered, finishing his coffee)

Thanks, boys. I think it's about time for my morning nap.
(They go off and come back and start setting up a camp cot downstage center.)
That was very good coffee, boys. Worth waiting for.

AIDES

Thanks, General.
(He lies down.)
Everything okay?

GENERAL

Everything that could be.
(They exit. The lights go out and a film is flashed on the screen. It is Africa on the March *and mainly depicts screaming hordes of Africans attacking various things, places, and people. Now and then the* GENERAL *moans in his sleep. The film switches to an apotheosis of the new, smiling Africa marching together in grand [1930s] style, then ends. After a moment the* GENERAL *awakens and rubs his eyes, then sits up and looks around.)*

GENERAL
(In a horrified tone)
Well, it's not MUCH, but it's a hell of a lot better than be-
ing THERE!

SCENE 12

(A rather decrepit nightclub [native-style] on a small Pacific
island. LUOA *is singing "Moon of Manakura" in her best*
Dorothy Lamour manner, while the GENERAL *is standing in*
the doorway. A self-conscious Chinese is standing beside him
as if waiting for him to order a drink. MRS. FORBES *is sitting*
at a table with BERT *and* EDGAR. *Toward the end of the song,*
LUOA *sings to the* GENERAL, *who looks away in embarrass-*
ment, only to encounter the gaze of MRS. FORBES *[politely in-*
terested] and BERT *and* EDGAR *[knowing]. He leaves when*
MRS. FORBES *smiles at him gaily.)*

BERT
How do you like that, the old goat.

EDGAR
I guess we caught him that time.

BERT
I wonder how he found out about this place.

EDGAR
It looked more like that singin' gal found out about him.

MRS. FORBES
(Not hearing them)
What a strange, forlorn face he has. It's rather tragic, I'd
say.

BERT
Not if you knew him.

34

MRS. FORBES

No, no. There's a future in that face; it has a peculiar, lonely strength. A future, and a terrible, mysterious past.

EDGAR

How about another drink, Mrs. Forbes?

MRS. FORBES

(Coming out of it)
You said it.

SCENE 13

(The GENERAL *is in a field of flowers. There are palm trees in the background and a sign in Chinese characters. He wanders about, admiring and sniffing, but not picking. He muses.)*

GENERAL

Hmmmm. I wonder if that's a gilly flower or a carnation. Oh well, what matter? One knows so little. And here's that crazy orchid that always reminds me of a seed catalog. When the adventure ceases to be speculation and becomes WORK . . . THEN boredom sets in. Then boredom sits down and tells you all about your activities in gray, greasy tones, tones like the sky over London on an average day. But what do I have against the British? The sweet William is a pretty flower, so there *can't* be anything *wrong* with England, any more than there can be anything *wrong* with Java or Bali. Well, but there may be something inherently wrong with any situation where beauty exists.

If it is true that the lily springs from the dung heap . . . then shouldn't we be offended by every place where beauty appears? Dung . . . animal dung, or the residue of our own human efforts? The question is vital. For if through our failures we can produce a beauty which has nothing to do with us, which is of a different nature from us, then that's pretty sinister. I mean, failure never produced a beautiful person, yet it might produce a beautiful flower . . . well, not a flower but a building, or a poem. For instance, the Taj Mahal is a failure—it doesn't house India's largest electrical corporation, does it, or the General Staff? No, no more than a poem gives you any information. I detest poems. Yet I can't deny they exist; indeed it's often relaxing to just leaf through a book of them without paying attention, like walking through this field of flowers. I don't admire them, they're just *there*. . . .I don't even smell much of anything. Now if this were a dung heap, I'd certainly smell *something!*

Shit, I never admired beautiful things, anyway. Never had time for them, never found them useful. The tragedy of architecture is: the only truly useful thing a building can do is let itself be bombed. Or just fall apart. Look at Angkor Wat. Everything on the face of this earth stays around too long. Of course, flowers decay faster than most things; maybe that's why I like them. But I don't admire them; I simply observe the wisdom of their disappearing sooner than, say, trees. . . .

Never liked children, either. They hang around, they grow up, they go on and on, and as adults they even cause more trouble than as kids. And they create crowds and then you feel crowded in. No, it's not nice, all that stuff. At least the flowers are only knee-high, so you don't notice how many of *them* there are.

(Enter MRS. FORBES.*)*

MRS. FORBES
(Noticing him after a moment)
Oh! I beg your pardon. I thought I heard people talking.

GENERAL

No, I am alone.

MRS. FORBES

Perhaps you wish to be alone.

GENERAL

Not particularly. Anyhow, it's an impossibility. . . . Anyhow, it's a public garden, so who am I to be alone in it?

MRS. FORBES

I'm Mrs. Forbes.

GENERAL

I'm a General.

MRS. FORBES

Yes, I know. I am acquainted with your adjutants.

GENERAL

They're my *aides*.

MRS. FORBES

I beg your pardon. You're not a very cheerful person, are you?

GENERAL

At times.
(Changing the subject)
What's that you're carrying?

MRS. FORBES

It's the poems of Rupert Brooke.

GENERAL

Can't abide the man. Or poetry either, for that matter.

MRS. FORBES
(Shyly)
Then perhaps it's I who should be alone.

GENERAL
(Crossly, but courteously)
Very well, madame.
(Exits)

MRS. FORBES
(After a moment, mysteriously)
Oh dear.

SCENE 14
(MRS. FORBES *being served coffee by a large Negro waiter in a sidewalk cafe.* BERT *and* EDGAR *and a girl enter.)*

MRS. FORBES
Boys! I think I'm in love!

EDGAR
It's the heat, Mrs. Forbes, the Malaysian heat. This is Constance.

MRS. FORBES
How do you do, Constance. I really do believe I am.

CONSTANCE
(Observing her closely)
I think you must be too, ducks.

BERT
(Bundling them off)
Let's get going. Here comes the rain!
(Sound of tropical outburst)

SCENE 15
(The lounge of a hotel, and the sound of rain outside. The same four are seated at table, and a waiter of Eurasian cast is taking orders.)

MRS. FORBES

I think I've had enough coffee for today.

(Turning to Constance)

Now tell me, my dear, arc you not the very girl we heard not long ago singing "Moon of Manakura"? Forgive me for my obtuseness.

CONSTANCE

Yes, I am Luoa. . . .

BERT

Yeah, we got her away from the General.

(MRS. FORBES *looks hurt.*)

CONSTANCE

. . . I found early in my career that where American soldiers were concerned the name Constance was far more advantageous than Luoa, though I *am* rather dark for a Constance.

EDGAR

No you're not.

MRS. FORBES

(Bravely)

Apparently I forgot to tell you who I'm in love *with*. Well, it's the General. The General in a field of flowers.

EDGAR

IMPOSSIBLE!

MRS. FORBES

He was! He absolutely *was*! I never talked with him anywhere else! You know that.

BERT

He means: it's impossible that you're in love with him.

MRS. FORBES

Oh!

(Suddenly beaming)

I know. Isn't it divine? To think! . . . In love again, me! In love again, and in love with a General again!

SCENE 16

(The hall of a marble palace. The GENERAL up a few steps from BERT and EDGAR, whom he is addressing.)

GENERAL

God, it's great to be back in Manila! You never thought I'd make it, did you?

BERT

Er . . . Ah . . .

EDGAR

Yes we did.

GENERAL

No you didn't.

EDGAR

Well we almost did.

GENERAL

(Purposefully)

Well, I don't give a damn whether you did or didn't. We're here anyway. And there's going to be a little reinstatement of discipline around here. You two have been lounging around the islands with your ladyfriends long enough. I want every square inch of marble in this palace shining like snow in the Arctic. Get some buckets and some brushes and some knee pads, and get to work for a change! That'll sweeten your tempers and take that smug look off your faces. Then when you're finished we'll have a little cloak-and-dagger maneuvers to keep you in training, *if* you can walk by then.

(They have come to attention as well as they can remember.)
Okay, dismissed.
(They exit.)

SCENE 17

(Taiwan, a terrace and a Chinese rose arbor in which sit the GENERALISSIMO and MME. CHIANG KAI-SHEK, apparently reading aloud to each other. The GENERALISSIMO interrupts her in the middle of the sentence: But for a long time she remembered the plangent sweetness of that far-off garden with a tenacity . . .)

GENERALISSIMO
A what?

MADAME
A tenacity.

GENERALISSIMO
Oh . . . By the way, I received a report this morning from our agent, Lin Foo.

MADAME
Good heavens! The General's not coming our way, is he?

GENERALISSIMO
No.

MADAME
What a relief! House guests are all very well, but *he's* a far cry from Mrs. Roosevelt.

GENERALISSIMO
Don't worry your pretty little head about it. Still . . . it is odd that he'd be in our neighborhood and then go all the way up to the Philippines without bothering us at all. I'm afraid it may mean that we've become rather déclassé, my dear.

MADAME

Better déclassé than a nervous wreck.
(A few scattered sounds of bombing)

GENERALISSIMO

That's my girl.

MADAME

How well I remember him at our commencement at Wellesley. So young, so dashing—it seemed the world was at his feet.

GENERALISSIMO

All well and good, but he didn't get to be a Generalissimo!

MADAME

(Fondly)

No, just a General, poor thing.

GENERALISSIMO

That's what comes of being born in the wrong place at the wrong time. I've always maintained that. It's Ying and Yang, I suppose.

MADAME

(Seriously)

You are a very wise man.

GENERALISSIMO

Thank you. I wish more people realized it.
(Bursting out)
Honestly, if they don't stop that bombing, I'm going to . . .

MADAME

No, darling, don't upset yourself. It will stop. As you always say, "Ying and Yang."

GENERALISSIMO

Well it better.

(Changing his mood)
Yes, yes. Now let me read you this delicious bit from *Vanity Fair*.

MADAME
Oh please!

SCENE 18

(A neon sign blinking "TOKYO NIGHTS" off and on.
CONSTANCE *and* MRS. FORBES *are drinking in the latter's hotel
room.* MRS. FORBES *in a maribou peignoir,* CONSTANCE *in her
singing costume.)*

MRS. FORBES
One thing I'll say for the Japanese, the liquor's cheaper
here.

CONSTANCE
I know, but I was really counting on that job. I'm telling
you, when that night-club manager said that to me back-
stage I got so mad I could have spit.

MRS. FORBES
(Surprised)
Constance! You wouldn't have!

CONSTANCE
I didn't. But I felt like it.

MRS. FORBES
Life takes its toll of one, doesn't it?

CONSTANCE
You know it's one of those situations which are so aggra-
vating that all one's principles, all the niceties one has
strived to maintain, just go up in smoke! I was flaming
mad!

43

MRS. FORBES

It does sound exciting.

CONSTANCE

Oh he was plenty excited all right. I was as cold as a cobra. If I'd been a cobra I'd have given him a good bite on his fat finger.

MRS. FORBES

Try to get your mind off it.

CONSTANCE

Oh I can't. I wasn't brought up for a life like this. I wasn't *equipped* for it. It's one thing to walk out of the palm grove onto a little wooden platform and start singing—but *le monde chic* is too much for this little girl. You can have it.

MRS. FORBES

No, dear. I have had it.

CONSTANCE

You're a wonderful person!

MRS. FORBES

No, I'm not. Not really.

CONSTANCE

And so modest.

MRS. FORBES

OH CUT IT OUT!
(CONSTANCE *is abashed.*)
Sorry, dear. You were reminding me of someone I once knew rather well.

CONSTANCE

Oh . . . That can be painful. . . .

44

MRS. FORBES

It's not that. . . . It's just that I miss the General so much.

CONSTANCE

Poor baby. Say! I miss those boys an awful lot too. Why don't we fly up and see them? I'm broke, but if you could lend me the fare I'd pay you back when I get a job in Manila.

MRS. FORBES

Oh dear. I really don't *have* enough. It was so expensive buying my way out of Bandung.

CONSTANCE

Yeah. Oh it's silly for me to think of going anyway. I don't love them, I just like them.

MRS. FORBES

And yet, when I think of his stern face above those nodding flowers, the very figure of a General before his troops . . . No, no. It would be too painful. And he's probably forgotten me already. . . . What am I saying! He never even knew me! How silly.

CONSTANCE

We're probably better off here. And tomorrow I'm going to go out and get some money.

MRS. FORBES

I wouldn't do *that,* dear, it ruins your looks. There must be another way.

SCENE 19

(An airport waiting room. A large sign says "SCHIZO-DROME—ROUTES EAST AND WEST." BERT *and* EDGAR *are disheveled and staring accusingly at the* GENERAL.*)*

GENERAL
(Shouting)
. . . AND FURTHERMORE, HOW DID I KNOW
THEY WANTED THE DAMN PALACE BACK!

SCENE 20
*(A village square in Borneo, surrounded by verdure and in
the distance the deep blue hills of Borneo. The* GENERAL *and*
AIDES *walk on, as if taking a morning constitutional.)*

GENERAL
Back to Borneo. Little did I think that cry would ever
strike a responsive chord in my breast.

BERT
Yeah, Chief. We always kept bypassing Borneo before.

EDGAR
We let the Aussies take it—but I think it's *nice.*
(A group of NATIVES *appear and salaam and carry on gener-
ally.)*

GENERAL
Yes indeed, and here they know who a person *is,* too.
(To natives)
I'm back, you see.

NATIVES
(Enthusiastically)
Hooray!
(They exit.)

GENERAL
Yes indeed.
(To AIDES*)*
A charming lot.

BERT

They've got no hard feelings.

EDGAR

Why should they? We've never been here before.

GENERAL

Yes indeed.

(MRS. FORBES *enters.*)

MRS. FORBES

Well for heaven's sakes!

BERT AND EDGAR

Hi, Mrs. Forbes!

GENERAL
(Warily)

Good day to you. What are you doing here?

MRS. FORBES
(Embarrassed)

Uhh . . .

BERT

Yeah, Mrs. Forbes, what are you doing in this neck of the woods?

MRS. FORBES
(Bravely)

I was . . . running away.

EDGAR
(Solicitously)

You're not in any danger, are you?

BERT
(Solicitously)

Who are you running away from?

MRS. FORBES
(Delicately confused)

I guess . . . I was just running away . . . from life! Oh I
think things can get pretty painful sometimes, don't you?

GENERAL
(Reassured)

That sounds pretty silly to me. Running away from life!

MRS. FORBES
(Sadly)

I suppose you're right.

EDGAR
(Relieved)

So that's all it was! Say, what ever happened to Constance?

MRS. FORBES

Oh I left *her* in Tokyo. She was frightfully busy.

BERT

Busy doing what?

MRS. FORBES

I don't know, just busy. Besides, I found out she's a spy for
Chiang Kai-shek. Can you imagine? Her real name is Lin
Foo and they hardly pay her a cent for all her spying, so she
has to keep busy on her own.

GENERAL

Well that beats everything!

MRS. FORBES
(Eager to have his attention)

You don't know the half of it! Would you believe it: they
don't even pay for her coded cablegrams with all the information. The poor girl has to go out and hus . . . and
work to pay for them!

EDGAR

It's despicable!

GENERAL

Well, I don't like spies. Never had any use for them.
(Looking meaningfully at MRS. FORBES*)*
I think it serves her right.

BERT

(Aside to EDGAR*)*
Of course *he* called them *scouts.*

MRS. FORBES

(Eagerly)
I'm sure that's the sensible way to look at it. But she's such
a lovely girl, except for that one fault.

GENERAL

Yes, I suppose she is.
(Genially and appealingly)
And a girl has to earn living, doesn't she?

MRS. FORBES

Exactly. Oh General, you're so open! So fair!

GENERAL

(Beaming)
I try to be; yes indeed, I do try to be.

MRS. FORBES

(Afraid her infatuation is showing)
Well . . . I'd better be getting along and see to my luggage
and lodgings. I just popped off the plane and went out for
a stroll. . . . I suppose you military people call it recon-
noitering? . . . Ha ha ha . . .

GENERAL

What? Not at all!

(To AIDES*)*

You boys run along to the airport and pick up Mrs. Forbes's luggage, then engage a room for her at our hotel.

(To MRS. FORBES*)*

That will do, won't it?

(She nods. To AIDES *again)*

Run along, now! Hop to it!

(They exit rapidly.)

MRS. FORBES

Oh, thank you. You're awfully kind to look after me. I find travel so confusing, though I do it all the time.

GENERAL

Yes, yes. Of course you do.

(Thinking for a moment, then offering his arm)

Now . . . what say we take a little stroll through Borneo? Who knows, we may find another field of flowers . . . and this time we'll settle down and have a good long talk.

(The NATIVES *start entering again, inquisitively.)*

Would you enjoy that?

MRS. FORBES

(After a moment, incredulously)

Oh, I'd love it!

GENERAL

(After a moment, possessively)

Well come along then.

(He leads her off as:)

NATIVES

(Severally)

HOORAY! HOORAY! HOORAY!

SCENE 21

(Same scene, and following quickly on the last. BERT *and* EDGAR *enter loaded down with luggage of a bizarre and heterogeneous nature, difficult to grasp. They are puffing with exertion, so there are short pauses as they struggle across.)*

BERT

Well . . . *something's* happening at last!

EDGAR

(Gasping)

Nobody else knows who he *is*!

NATIVES

(Reappearing, very cheerful, dancing)

GO HOME YANQUI!

*(*MRS. FORBES *rushes on distraught.)*

MRS. FORBES

Oh God! the most awful thing has happened!

(She pauses hysterically. They drop all the bags.)

Oh and we were going to be so happy together, I know we were, and now this! . . .

(More quietly)

We walked out into the field of flowers. Everything around was radiant with promise. My eyes were shining, his eyes were shining, my heart was pounding, his . . .

(Screams, then recovers)

No, it couldn't have been his heart, it was his . . . his . . . lungs. I knew he was going to say, "I love you," when all of a sudden he got all choked up. At first I thought it was perfectly appropriate, you know, I slapped him on the back. Then he keeled over into the flowers and died. He couldn't get his breath! It was awful! It *is* awful.

(She staggers.)
I'm afraid I feel a little faint. . . .
(Two natives grab her as she collapses. BERT *and* EDGAR *rush to her side.)*

BERT

God! he never did that before.

EDGAR

Well of course not, you dope. You only *can* do that *once!*

BERT

I mean he was never allergic to flowers. I guess it was psychosomatic!

EDGAR

He was a great man, *too great* to be domesticated.

BERT

I guess he *was* a great man *once.*

NATIVES
(Not comprehending)
GO HOME YANQUI!

THE END

CAFFE CINO

JOSEPH CINO, owner of the Caffe Cino.

The Caffe Cino opened in December 1958 as a coffeehouse, with no plan to present plays. Soon we made time and space available for occasional poetry readings. Actors needing a place to perform gravitated to the cafe, gave staged readings on slow nights, then full productions. For the past five years the Caffe Cino has presented a regular schedule of plays, usually the work of new playwrights, usually for a run of one or two weeks. *The Madness of Lady Bright* is the only play to date that has had an extended run at the Cino.

It's a very small room and there's no time ever to think about expanding or where you go from here—after eight years. The work has been endless. We try to change the feeling of the room as much as possible to go with the current production. When it works it's very rewarding. It's never really planned, but somehow we make it happen within that 24-hour changeover between productions.

The best things happen when the entire company works together with concern for the entire production. The attitudes vary a great deal, but the best rhythm is when the entire company is completely involved with the production, on stage and off.

I decide on everything that comes into the room. I talk to playwrights, I talk to directors. I work with people. I work by intuition much more than by reading scripts. Sometimes I will realize after a night or two that a play is very bad. I could easily stop it and get something else. But everything plays its full run. Many people attack me for this, and probably many people stay away because of it. Only once did I cancel a show, and that was mutually agreed upon by the whole company. I remember a whole series of works that turned out to be nothing at all, and we went on night after night with almost no one here. But that passed.

The thing I've been thinking about is how to be more selective. It's the most difficult thing of all. Sometimes I've let people do things here for no particular reason and their work has turned out to be very special. Certain people have had periods when they did things that were very high, but they're just not doing anything imaginative now. And there are a few people who come in year after year wanting to work here and I always say no. I like to feel that we're open to everything, but I don't like to feel that the stage is being used simply for abuse or to be shocking. Since we reopened in May 1965, after the fire, just about everything we've done has been exciting.

When I now go see something on a proscenium stage it's like something else—with no comparisons to what is done here. But this is a theatre, a mirror of all the madness of everything else that is happening. Every evening I have actors and writers and directors phoning and coming in about working here. It's never-ending. One dancer sends people here: "You must go there and have their eggs. By the way, they do plays also."

It's very rewarding to sit here alone after closing or in the afternoon, collecting myself and my thoughts around the room. It's very small, but there's everything here, and it keeps moving. Every day it keeps happening. And it's always different.

The Madness of Lady Bright

by Lanford Wilson

THE MADNESS OF LADY BRIGHT was first presented at the Caffe Cino on May 19, 1964. It was directed by Denis Deegan with sets by Joseph Davies, lighting by John Torrey, and had the following cast:

LESLIE BRIGHT_____Neil Flanagan

GIRL_____Carolina Lobravico

BOY_____Eddie Kenmore

The production was revised with new casts and a redirection by William Archibald to run a total of 168 performances at the Cino.

LANFORD WILSON *was born in Lebanon, Missouri, on April 13, 1938. He graduated from high school in Ozark, Missouri, and attended college at San Diego State and the University of Chicago. He arrived in New York in the summer of 1962 and discovered the Caffe Cino about six months later. Since then he has had eleven productions at the Cino and four (including* Balm in Gilead, *a full length play) at Cafe La Mama. Theatre 1965 presented his* Home Free! *at the Cherry Lane Theatre on the first bill of their New Playwrights' Series. The play has since been translated into eight languages. Other Off-Broadway productions include two at Theatre East,* The Madness of Lady Bright *and* Ludlow Fair, *and* This Is the Rill Speaking, *presented by the La Mama Repertory Company at the Martinique Theatre. Hill and Wang have published his* Balm in Gilead and Other Plays. *Mr. Wilson is a member of the Actors Studio Playwrights' Unit and the New Dramatists Committee.*

The Madness of Lady Bright

by Lanford Wilson

For Neil Flanagan

CHARACTERS: LESLIE BRIGHT, *a man of about forty; he is a screaming preening queen, rapidly losing a long-kept "beauty."* THE BOY *and* THE GIRL: *Both are very attractive, perhaps twenty-five, dressed in dark, simple, casual clothes.*

SCENE

(The stage within a stage is set as LESLIE BRIGHT'S *one-room apartment. The walls are light and covered over with hundreds of signatures, or autographs, mostly only names, in every conceivable size and writing medium. The name "Adam" is prominent on one wall, on another is "Michael Delaney." There is a dresser with nail polish, hair brush, lipstick, various clutter across the top. A desk, chair, papers, telephone. A portable phonograph that works passably well and records. The room seems tucked like a pressing book with mementos, post cards, letters, photographs, pictures of men from body-building magazines. A bed with pink and white silk sheets is against one wall. A window looks out to the back of buildings across the back yard below, a scene like the seventies between Amsterdam and Columbus avenues in upper Manhattan. The room is very sunny. A hot, still summer afternoon.*

The characters of the BOY *and* GIRL *are used to move the action—to* LESLIE'S *memories, moods—they express, as actors,*

59

various people, voices, lovers. Sometimes they should be involved, sometimes almost bored, impatient, sometimes openly hostile, as the people he has known.

At curtain the three walk on and assume their positions. The BOY *and* GIRL *sit to the side, or either side;* LESLIE, *entering, carrying a telephone, in character, sits at the desk and dials a number. After a moment of half-listening, a double-take, he turns to the couple.)*

LESLIE

(Broadly)

Do you *know* what is comforting the world on Dial-A-Prayer this abysmally hot Saturday afternoon?

GIRL

(Prefatorily, to the audience)

Abysmally Hot Saturday Afternoon . . .

LESLIE

(Cutting in, superior)

You think lately perhaps you've been overly preoccupied with sex; you should turn to deeper, more solemn matters, and Dial-A-Prayer gives you: "The Lord is my Shepherd, I shall not want. He maketh me to LIE DOWN in green pastures." God, what an image. Out in a green pasture, yet. Well, Adam, if that isn't heaven. . . . Why didn't you maketh me to lie down in green pastures, Adam? Why didn't you just maketh me to lie down? Why didn't you maketh me?

(He has been looking through an address book.)

Well, who would be home?

(Dials)

Stalwart queen, I can't believe even you would walk the street in this heat.

(Hanging up)

One day you're going to melt into the sidewalk
(Looking through the book)
into this little puddle of greasy rouge and nylons.
(Dials)
Ring. Ring.
(Holds telephone receiver between his shoulder and ear, picks up the bottle of nail polish and polishes one nail.)
Ring.
(Looking at the hand)
Ten rings, dear, that's enough for any girl. One for every finger. Cheap damn Chinese red. Junk. No one. No one is home.
(Waving hand to dry)
That's ten, sweetheart—okay, one extra for the index finger—eleven, that's all, sorry.
(Hangs up sloppily)
So, no one is home.

BOY
You're home.

LESLIE
(Cutting in)
I'm home, of course. Home.
(Looks around)
Oh, god! Well, face it, girl; you'll drive yourself stiff if you can't find someone else to drive. . . .
(He fans through the address book)
Oh, to hell with you.
(Tossing it aside)
You bore me.
(Affected voice)
You bore me!
(Rather seriously)
You are a pile of paper addresses and memories, paper

phone numbers and memories, and you mean nothing to me.

(Trying to catch the line just said)

You—I am surrounded—I am left with

(Rather desperately trying to catch the right phrasing of the line to write it down)

a—with paper memories and addresses. . . .

(Finds a piece of paper at the desk, with a pencil, bent over the desk)

I am—how?

BOY

I am left with a—with paper memories.

GIRL

With paper addresses.

BOY

You are a pile of addresses and remembrances.

LESLIE

How did it go?

GIRL

(Singing)

Memories, memories.

LESLIE

How did it go?

BOY

I am a paper.

LESLIE

Oh, to hell with it. I should go out.

(Looking at the polished nail)

If nothing else in the world, I am certain that that is the wrong color for me.

(Sitting down)

I—I—

(Totally different thought)

I should never wear anything other than blue. Aqua. The color of the sea.

(Rising)

I am Venus, rising from . . . and matching eye shadow. And nothing else.

(He looks in the mirror for the first time. Stops. Looks bitchily at his reflection)

You. Are a faggot. There is no question about it any more— you are definitely a faggot. You're funny but you're a faggot.

(Pause)

You have *been* a faggot since you were four years old. Three years old.

(Checking the mirror again)

You're not *built* like a faggot—necessarily. You're built like a disaster. But, whatever your dreams, there is just no possibility whatever of your ever becoming, say, a lumberjack. You know?

(He has risen, wandering aimlessly about the room.)

GIRL

You know?

(Music, very softly from outside)

LESLIE

I know. I just said it. None whatever. Oh, you're spinning around in your stupid room like Loretta Young for Christsake. You should have a long circular skirt and . . .

(Long stretching motion with his arm as he turns, imitating Loretta Young's television entrance)

"Hello. John?"

(He stops. They all hear the music now, a Mozart concerto, very faint.)

Why, how lovely.

GIRL

How soft, distant. Isn't that lovely?

BOY

It is.
(The three drift toward the window.)

LESLIE

It must be coming from someone's apartment. Some faggot's apartment.
(They are at the window.)
He's turned on the Bach—no, it's Mozart. And he's preparing dinner nervously, with some simple salad and some complex beef stew. And they'll dine by candlelight and ruin their eyes. Sometimes in summer it seems the only way to remain sane is listening to the radios playing in the neighborhood. I haven't a radio myself; I discovered I was talking back to it so I kicked it out. I have only the phonograph you saw and some worn-out records.
(The BOY and GIRL have become visitors.)

GIRL

The music is lovely.

BOY

Where's it coming from, can you tell?

LESLIE

I don't know. Somewhere. It's nice at a distance like that. Sometimes in summer it seems the only way to remain sane is by listening to—of course, it's a mixed neighborhood. Oh, well. I get Spanish guitars and a good deal of Flamenco music as well. Of course I enjoy that too. At a distance like that.

GIRL

So soft, like that.

64

BOY

It's all right.

(They turn from the window.)

LESLIE

Mozart has always been one of my favorites; I know, you'll say how *or*dinary, but Mozart and Bach, I believe they have —oh, I don't know. It's so immature to try to analyze music. *(The window has become the doorway to a symphonic hall; they exit, moving away slowly, and* LESLIE *lights a cigarette, as at intermission.)*

BOY

It isn't necessary to talk about it; you just listen to it.

LESLIE

Exactly. I know. But they'll intellectualize and say that *this* is like a sunset and *that*—I mean it's so phoney.

GIRL

It is.

LESLIE

I get really passionately upset by that sort of thing. Music is not like a sunrise, it's like *(They are laughing at his joke before it is finished.)* *music,* isn't it? I mean, isn't it?

GIRL

That's so true.

BOY

That's true.

(They walk away. LESLIE *remains standing in the same position. The music has faded away.)*

LESLIE

(Continuing)

I go to these concerts only to listen to the music, not to see the white cliffs of wherever-it-is. I only . . .

(Listens)

It's stopped.

(Goes to window again)

Why do you always hear that stupid concerto, the same one? There is no one out there who would have been playing it, is there?

(To the walls)

Is there, Autographs?

(Listens)

What was that?

(This is bawdy—Judy Garland yelling to her doting audience.)

What was that once more?

(Big)

We'll stay all night and sing 'em all!

(A bow)

(Drops his cigarette)

God damn! Burn the place down.

BOY
(Correcting; this exchange rapidly, with almost sadistic inanity)

Up.

GIRL

Burn the place *up.*

LESLIE

Up or down?

GIRL

Up or down.

BOY
(Echo)

Up or down?

LESLIE

Down or up?

(LESLIE *sits at dresser.*)

GIRL

(Cutting in)

You're so damn sloppy; if you've got to smoke . . .

LESLIE

(Cutting in)

I don't *have* to smoke, I *prefer* to smoke.

GIRL

(Cutting in)

Got to smoke you could at least take a few elementary precautions not to burn the place down.

BOY

Up.

GIRL

Not to burn the place up.

LESLIE

(Cutting in)

I am a very nervous person and I have to have something to do with my hands and I PREFER to smoke, if you don't mind! If you don't MIND!

GIRL

Well, you can buy your own cigarettes; don't expect me to supply cigarettes for you, and don't think I don't notice when you steal mine.

LESLIE

I wouldn't touch yours. . . .

GIRL

You can march down to the store and buy your own—if you're not ashamed to be seen there.

(The BOY *has laughed chidingly at "march.")*

LESLIE

Why would I be . . .

(Breaks off, turns to mirror)

Hmm.

(Hands to sides of eyes, testily)

Oh, not good. Not good at all. All those spidery little wrinkles showing your *A-G-E*. Exposing yourself, aren't you? And a gray hair or two—and your whole face just collapsing. Built like a disaster.

(Turning mirror away)

Oh, do go away.

(To the back of mirror)

You should be preserved somewhere. You are a very rare specimen that should be saved for posterity. *Lowered* into the La Brea tar pits in a time capsule as a little piece of the twentieth century that didn't quite come off. Along with an Olivetti typewriter and a can of—cream of celery soup.

(Turning mirror back again)

Whatever you're telling me I don't want to hear it. I've heard it before from every bitchy queen alive. The old fey mare ain't what she used to be. But she's well preserved, you've got to give her that. *A line or two,* but holding together. By a thread.

(Rising)

But she can sing like a nightingale. Well, nearly. And dance like Giselle. Giselle was a little willie—a willie is a fairy who dances in the woods.

(Almost as though telling a story to the BOY *and* GIRL*)*

And, well, they tried to make Giselle's husband dance all night and she danced all night in his place.

(Aside)

Didn't you, Giselle? You did. You saved his life.

(To the walls)

Now, what have I done for you? All my visitors—all the men who have visited this stupid apartment for the last ten or so years—what have I ever done for you? Well, let's face it, what did you ever do for me? Look at it that way. Precious little.

(Jumping onto the bed, tapping a finger against a crossed-out name)

Oh, you! Quentin! I scratched your name off over a year ago; you gave me—what particular social disease was it you gave me? You with your neat little signature. Tight, like-a-spring-little-signature. You can always tell a man by the way he signs his name, and a tight signature is very, very bad, Quentin.

BOY

How come?

LESLIE

(Walking away. Only mildly scolding)

I have studied graphology and believe me, it is very, very *bad*, Quentin. You will undoubtedly give me some dreadful social disease. And you, another meek little signature. In pencil. But you were only an edge bashful, only shy. For a meek little signature, Arnold Chrysler, you weren't really bad. You were not Adam, but there was only one. You were none of you like—anything like—Adam. Well, Michael Delaney was wonderful indeed; marvelous indeed, but he was not Adam.

(Cheek to Adam's name)

You were everything. You are what I remember. Always the dreams are you.

(Turning away, laughing)

Dreams? Oh, my dear. Fantasies. Oh, you are definitely cracking.

(Into mirror)

Mirror, you are—I am sorry to report—cracking up.

(Frustrated)

I am losing my mind. I am. I am losing my faggot mind. I'm going insane.

(The Mozart returns, but never important—very distantly, and only for a few bars.)

It's this stupid apartment and the goddamned heat and NO ONE EVER BEING AT HOME!

(To telephone)

Why don't you answer?

(To himself)

You are growing old and fat and insane and senile and old.

(Goes to phone, dials. Ends the nervous note, says with the phone:)

"The Lord is my"—yes, we know all that.

(Hangs up. Dials)

All of you are never, ever, ever at home.

(Looking about the room as the phone rings on and on)

YOU at least never had homes. You never lived in one place more than a week. Bums and vagabonds, all of you; even Adam, admit it. Tramp around the world, hustling your box from Bermuda to Bangkok! From Burma to Birmingham. How was Birmingham, Adam? What? Oh, don't lie to me, EVERYONE has hustled his box in Birmingham.

(Notices the phone is in his hand, hangs up)

Never home. At least you can count on Dial-A-Prayer being home.

(Tosses book on the desk)

70

You, you whores, tramp-the-street bitches. Dial-A-Prayer, and weather and the correct time and Pan American Airways travel information and TWA and American and Delta and Ozark—and the public library. You can count on—but an acquaintance? Don't count on it. There is no one outside.

(Laughs)

Well!

(To the BOY *and* GIRL*)*

A little action, huh?

(They laugh, party-like.)

I hate beer, just a coke, please: Yes, I know they're both fattening, you whore, I don't have to worry about that YET! Beauty isn't everything! . . . But then what is? Come on.

GIRL

Come on.

(A rock and roll record comes up.)

BOY

Come on. Let's dance.

LESLIE

Let's dance.

*(*GIRL *dances with* BOY, LESLIE *dances with imaginary partner. The* BOY *talks both for himself and* LESLIE'S *partner. But* LESLIE *doesn't know the dance.)*

What is it? What on earth? Oh, God, I couldn't do that. Zat new? Huh? Well tell me the steps anyway.

BOY

Zeasy.

LESLIE

Walk through it once.

BOY

Just follow.

LESLIE

I'll try. Oh, God.
(Catching on, but not completely getting it)

BOY

Zit.

LESLIE

Is it?
(They continue to dance, very fast, very tiring, until the end of the record and it goes off. General noise)

GIRL

Swell.

BOY

Thanks.
(They walk away.)

GIRL

Wheeh! It's so warm.

BOY

Yeah.

LESLIE

Is that all? Hell, it's over; put another quarter in. Ha!
(Comes out of it)
Goddamn. Every time, all over sweat. You crazy loon.
Stupid bitch. You should get dressed up and go down to the
beach, it's so damn muggy and hot they must need a little
something to liven up the beach about now.
*(Makes a quick single enormous cabbage rose of the top
sheet and puts it on his head as a fashionable hat—walks
across the room as in a beauty contest, singing lowly)*

"There she is; Miss America. . . ."
(Takes rose from head, holds it to cover himself—a vision of total nudity, raises his eyes to the imaginary judge's bench. With sunny brightness)
Good morning, Judge!
(Pause)
Your Honor.
(Tosses it aside, goes to dresser)
Oh, dear.
(Pause)

BOY
(They have been ignoring him. To the actress quietly, privately)
Did you go somewhere?

LESLIE
(Tossing the sheet back to the bed)
No.

GIRL
When?

BOY
Last night. Did you go out for a while?

GIRL
Oh, yes. I went for cigarettes.

BOY
I missed you. I rolled over for a second and stretched, you know—and you weren't there—and I thought where the hell—then I must have drifted off again. Got up and got dressed?

GIRL
I went out for a few minutes down to the drug store.

BOY

I wondered.

GIRL

It was raining.

BOY

(Faking a hurt voice)

Well, you might consider—I looked over expecting you to be there—and there was nothing but loneliness.

LESLIE

(To himself—listening in spite of himself.)

Loneliness.

(He is not looking toward them.)

GIRL

You were asleep when I came back.

BOY

It's a terrible thing to wake up to loneliness.

(LESLIE looks sharply toward him at the word repeated.)

GIRL

I came right back; it was wet as hell. You know?

LESLIE

You know nothing about loneliness.

(Long pause)

I should go out.

(Seeing name on the wall)

I should go out and look for you. . . .

(Creeping up on the name)

Mich-ael De-lan-ey—

(Grabbing the wall)

Gotcha!

(Turning from the wall)

74

Good Lord—eight years ago—you would be how old by now? Oh well, old hustlers never die, they just start buying it back!

(Turning back to the wall)

You were very good, I remember that. And who else?

(Going over the names)

So-so; fair; clumsy, but cute anyway; too intelligent; Larry; good, I remember; A minus, and that's very good; undersized; very nice; *over*sized, but I'm not complaining.

(Suddenly angry)

Samuel Fitch!

(Runs to the desk for a pencil)

Samuel Fitch!

(Scratches the name off)

No, I thought you were gone! You bitch! You liar! You vicious faggot! You QUEER! You were not a man, you were some worm. Some smelly worm.

(Feeling better)

Of course, you couldn't help it, you were BORN a worm. Once a worm always a worm, I always say.

(Looking back at the erased name)

Oh. Poor Samuel. You really couldn't help it, could you? You were queer but you couldn't help it. Domineering mother probably. What was it—that was sweet—you said. You said my body was smooth.

(The Mozart is back, softly but getting louder.)

Hairless, that's what you liked about it. You said I moved well, too, didn't you? Well, I DO move well. I move EXCEPTIONALLY well.

(Sits on the side of the bed. Giselle music is added to the Mozart, and in a moment the rock and roll also joins.)

And I haven't a hair on my body. I'm as hairless and smooth as a newborn babe. I shave, of course, my underarms; no

woman would go around with hair under her arms. It's just
not done. Lately. In America anyway.

(Stretches his legs.)

And my legs—they're smooth. They are.

(Feeling the backs of his legs)

I have—I

(Nervously)

I have varicose veins in my legs. I can't wear hose. I have
hideous, dreadful legs. I have blue, purple, BLACK veins
in my legs. They give me pain—they make me limp, they
ache, they're ugly. They used to be beautiful and they are
bony and ugly. Old veins.

(The BOY *and* GIRL *begin to rub their legs and arms and to
moan low.)*

Old legs, dancing legs; BUT THE VEINS! They get tired.
And when they get

(Fast)

old they get tired and when they get tired they get slow
and when they get slow they get stiff and when they get stiff
they get brittle and when they get brittle they break and the
veins break and your bones snap and your skin sags. . . .
The veins in my arms and legs—my veins are old and brittle and the arteries break—your temples explode your veins
break like glass tubes—you can't walk you can't dance you
can't speak; you stiffen with age. Age takes you over and
buries you; it buries you under—under—MY VEINS, my
arms, my body, my heart, my old callused hands; my ugly
hands; my face is collapsing. I'm losing my mind.

(The BOY *finally screams a long, low* Oh. *The* GIRL *screams
nervously* I'm going insane.*)*

I'm going insane. I'm going insane!

BOY

My veins, my arteries.

(The BOY *and* GIRL *speak the next two lines simultaneously.)*

GIRL
I'm being buried.

BOY
I'm old; I'm growing old.

GIRL
(Singing)
Memories, memories.
(The music has now reached its loudest point.)

LESLIE
(Speaking over GIRL's *singing)*
I'm losing my MIND. I'M LOSING MY MIND. OH, GOD, I'M LOSING MY MIND!
(He falls panting onto the bed. The only music left is the Mozart, very far away. After a moment he gets up. He notices his pants leg is pulled up; he slowly pulls it down.)
I. . . .

GIRL
(Chattering madly)
If you must smoke you could at least buy your own.

BOY
How did it go, memories and paper and addresses on the walls and . . . ?

GIRL
And don't tell me . . .

LESLIE
(Sits on side of the bed. To himself)
I should.

GIRL
And don't tell me you don't snatch mine; I've seen you. I

sometimes count them, you know. Did you ever think about that?

LESLIE

I—I should go out.
(Rises, walks to desk, sits)
That way insanity, Leslie. That way the funnyfarm, Lady Bright. The men in white, Mary. And watch it, because you know you look like a ghost in white. You have never, ever worn white well.
(Rising)
You should never be seen in any color other than pink. Candy pink. Candy pink and white candy stripes. Silk.

GIRL

Well, of course.

LESLIE

(Walking toward the window)
Someone is playing their radio; I wonder what station plays Mozart all day long.
(The BOY has moved to beside the bed. He is buckling his belt.)
I know you don't understand it, but I do. Your pants are on the chair.

BOY

Yeah, I found them. You're good, I'll say that.

LESLIE

(Pleased)
Sometimes I just like to stand and listen to the music from someone's radio. I've done that a lot this summer. I live alone.
(He continues to look out the window, away from the BOY.)

BOY

I said you're good.

LESLIE

Well, of course. You see the names. Did you notice the names on the wall?

BOY

(Seeing them)

Yeah. I mean I see them now. You do it?

LESLIE

Of course not! They're autographs. No one has refused me. And I'll want yours, too, of course.

BOY

My what?

LESLIE

Your name, your autograph.

BOY

On the wall?

LESLIE

Yes. Whenever you want to write it. There's an ink pen on the table if you haven't one.

BOY

(Finding it and going to the wall.)

Yeah. Okay, you got it.

LESLIE

Don't tell me where. Move away now.

(He turns.)

Now.

(Surveying the walls)

There. Oh, so large, you egoist; it surely wasn't difficult to find it. Michael Delaney. You're Irish?

BOY

Yeah.

LESLIE

Irish.

(Distantly disappointed)

Well, it isn't romantic, is it? It's not Russian or Sicilian or one of those, but I've got nothing against the Irish. Any more. You have raised my opinion of them, I'll admit, considerably.

(The BOY *walks away, sits down.)*

I thought you only drank a good deal, but I find you have a capacity for other things as well. And it's just as well to add a favorite nationality; I was guessing you as Jewish; you don't mind me saying that—the dark hair, you know—but with a name like Michael Delaney you couldn't be anything else.

(The music has faded slowly out. LESLIE *looks out the window again)*

They've turned the radio down so I can't hear it now. I tell you,

(A quick glance at the name)

Michael, it's no fun. It's no fun living here in this stupid apartment by myself listening to my few records and the neighbor's radio; I should like someone, I think sometimes,

(Being delicate)

living here some times. Or maybe somehow not living here but coming here to see me often. Then I'd wash the walls—wash off everyone else. Wash them off and kiss them good-bye—good riddance. I've even thought I wouldn't mind, you know, just letting someone live here, scot free; I could prepare the meals—and do things. I—want to *do* things for someone who could live here. And he could sleep here, every night. It's really lovely—or would be—with the music. I'd like something like that, it

(Turning)

gets so lonely here by . . .

80

(But of course, he's gone. LESLIE *glances at the* BOY *sitting. To the* GIRL*)*

This dumb room.

(To the walls)

Dumb! Mute! All you goddamned cobwebby corners you stare down at me while I die of boredom; while I go insane because everyone I call is gone off somewhere. Once more.

(Goes to phone, dials, listens to the ringing)

Once. Twice. Thrice. Quadrice. Screw.

(Limply he puts his finger on the cradle, clicking off. Raises it and dials from memory another number)

GIRL

Good afternoon, American Airlines. May we help you?

LESLIE

Yes.

(Pause)

Fly me away from here.

(Clicks her off, leaving his finger on the phone. Long pause. Reflecting, bitchily)

Oh, well, fly yourself, fairy; you've got the wings. All God's chil'un got wings, Leslie. That's your disastrous body: wings and ass.

BOY

You've got a nice body. You know, a young body. How old are you, about nineteen?

*(*LESLIE *is surprised, almost stunned by the line. The* BOY *repeats the cue)*

How old are you, about nineteen?

(The BOY *has entered the room.)*

LESLIE

(Sadly; remembering)

Twenty.

(The scene now is played with young, fresh buoyancy.)
And you're what? The same age about, aren't you?

BOY

Twenty-one. Get drunk legally, any state.

LESLIE

I've never—I'm almost embarrassed—I've never met anyone as—well, I'm never at a loss for words, believe me. I
don't know what you have—anyone so good looking as you
are.
(BOY *laughs*)
What do you do? Are you a weight lifter?

BOY

Who—me? I don't do nothing. Bum around.

LESLIE

Bum around.

BOY

Been in every state.

LESLIE

Just bumming around?

BOY

One state pays for the next, you know?

LESLIE

You hustle, I guess. I mean—do you only hustle? I . . .

BOY
(Cutting in)
That's right. Oh, well, for kicks, too; sometimes. Why not?
When the mood hits me.

LESLIE

I wish to God it would hit you about now.

BOY

Yeah. Rough night, kid. Sorry.

LESLIE

Oh.

BOY

(Looking around)

Come on, they'll be other nights. I said I like you; you're a nice kid. We'll make it. I'll promise you.

LESLIE

You will?

BOY

I'll promise you that.

LESLIE

Good. Then I'll wait.

BOY

How long you been in this pad?

LESLIE

About a month. Everything's new. I painted the walls myself.

BOY

You ever seen one of these?

LESLIE

What? A grease pencil? Sure, I used to work in the china department of this stupid store; we marked dishes with them.

BOY

Mind if I do something?

LESLIE

What am I supposed to say?

(Earnestly)

No. I don't mind if you do something. Anything.

BOY

Something to remember me by.
(Goes to wall)

LESLIE

What? WHAT? Are you writing—your name? Hey, on my
fresh wall?
(The BOY *turns smilingly to him.)*
What the hell, it looks good there.

BOY

Yeah. I'll see you around.

LESLIE

Where are you going?
(No answer. LESLIE *is in the present now. The* BOY *walks to
his chair and sits.)*
Where are you going? Not you. Don't leave now. Don't.
Adam. You're not leaving. Come back here, don't go away;
you were the one I wanted. The only one I wanted, Adam!
Don't go away!
(Wildly)
Don't go, Adam; don't go, Adam.

GIRL

Unrequited love is such a bore.

BOY

Sad.

GIRL

Left him flat, didn't he?

BOY

The only one he wanted.

LESLIE

Oh, God, that way, honey, is madness for sure. Think about Adam and you've had it, honey. Into the white coat with the wrap-around sleeves.

(The following dialogue between the BOY *and* GIRL *takes place simultaneously with* LESLIE'S *next speech.)*

GIRL

It's sad, really.

BOY

It is. It really is. The only one he wanted really was Adam.

GIRL

And he never had him.

BOY

Never saw him after that.

GIRL

Of course he would have gone mad either way, don't you think?

BOY

Oh, yes.

GIRL

Drove himself to it, I mean. He couldn't have possibly lived a sane life like that.

BOY

Some pansies live a sane life and some don't. Like anyone else, I suppose.

GIRL

Well, not exactly.

BOY

I mean some go nuts and some don't. Some just go insane.

GIRL

Mad.

BOY

Nuts.

GIRL

Lose their balance, you know.

LESLIE

(Over the above. Moves to the record player and goes through the records, finds one.)

What I should have is some music. I'm so sick of music for companionship. But it's better than

(Looks to the telephone)

you queens! Never at home sick queens!

(Puts a record on. It is Judy Garland, singing a fast, peppy number. The volume is kept very low.)

Now that's better. That's a little better. I can dance to that one.

(He dances, as with a partner, but he dances a slow, sexy number as the music continues fast.)

There. I like the way you . . . Oh, you think I follow well. I'm glad you think I follow—I have a good sense of rhythm, I've always been told that I move well. I get lonely, but I've been told I move well. I sometimes just stare at the corners of my room, would you believe that, AND PRAY

(He stops dancing and stands still.)

AND PRAY FOR . . .

(Stops, panting)

I want—I WANT . . .

(But he can't say it.)

GIRL

(With comic remove)

He wants to die, I believe.

BOY

I think that's what he's trying to say.

GIRL

Well, it's easy to understand; I mean you couldn't expect him to live like that.

BOY

He's effeminate.

GIRL

No one can want to live if they're like that.

BOY

It's all right on girls.

LESLIE

Why do you let me live if you know it?

GIRL

(To BOY*)*
What could we do?

LESLIE

Why?

BOY

No one should live who's like that.

LESLIE

Giselle. Giselle, you saved him. You danced all night and you danced till dawn and you saved him. You did, you saved him; you danced for him. They let you save him.

GIRL

He used to be an intelligent fellow.

BOY

He was. He was a bright kid.

GIRL

Quick-thinking.

LESLIE

Why do you let me live if you know it? Can't you see I'm going insane alone in my room, in my hot lonely room? Can't you see I'm losing my mind? I don't want to be the way I am.

GIRL

He doesn't like the way he is.

BOY

He'd like to be different.

GIRL

He looks different enough to me.

BOY

Extraordinary, I'd say.

LESLIE

You could have killed me as a child, you could have.

GIRL

Christ! How can you play those goddamned records? Do you have to blare that MUSIC? DO YOU? YOU DANCE AROUND IN YOUR ROOM ALL DAY. Do something worth while why don't you?

LESLIE

You could have.

GIRL

Do something worth while.

LESLIE

(As before to Michael Delaney)

88

I'd like to do something.
(Suddenly)
No. We won't have this music.
(He's wild now, excited.)
We won't have this music.
(Strip music comes in over the Garland.)
We'll have a party. We'll have a show. I'll give you a show!

BOY

He's going to give you a show. I think.

GIRL

Turn that off!
(LESLIE goes to music. He turns it by accident to full volume, gets nervous, scratches the needle all the way across the record, at full volume. It clicks off. The other music goes off too.)

LESLIE
(Turning to them)
What would you like?

BOY
(To GIRL)
What would you like?

GIRL
(To LESLIE)
What would you like?

LESLIE
(Happily)
Oh, me! God. I—would—like . . . We won't have a show, we'll have a royal dance; a cotillion; a nice beautiful dance.

GIRL
A ball! Wonderful!

BOY

Lady Bright requests your presence . . .

LESLIE

A beautiful party.
(Grabs the sheet and winds it around him)

BOY

May I have the pleasure?

GIRL

I hardly know what to say.
(Mozart music comes up.)

LESLIE

And I shall be the queen! I dance with the most grace. I will be selected queen by popular demand. I dance like a flower on the water.
(Mozart up. They dance around in a whirl.)
I dance like a flower. I shall dance with Adam and you shall dance with whom you please. No, I have no more room on my program, I am dreadfully sorry, young man . . .
(Still dancing)
I am dancing tonight with only one man, you know what that means.

GIRL

She's so lovely.

BOY

She's so beautiful.

GIRL

Did you catch her name?

LESLIE

My name is Giselle! I am Giselle!
(Running to mirror)
I'm the fairest at the ball. I am the loveliest. I AM

YOUNG. I AM YOUNG AND LOVELY. YES, I AM YOUNG!

(He bends over the dressing table and returns to the mirror. He takes up lipstick and smears it across his lips, half his face.)

I am young tonight. I will never be old. I have all my faculties tonight.

(The people have continued to dance. LESLIE returns and they whirl about. Other music joins the Mozart—Giselle, the rock and roll, the strip number.)

I am beautiful. I am happy!

(LESLIE falls down. They continue to dance about him. The music stops. Then comes on. Stops. Returns. A pulsating effect)

LESLIE

Excuse me, I must have . . .

(Music continues loudly.)

My arms are so tired. My legs. I have bad legs; I don't walk too well. The veins in my legs are getting old, I guess. . . .

(This is light, chattery talk.)

I grow tired easily. I GROW BRITTLE AND I BREAK. I'M LOSING MY MIND, YOU KNOW. EVERYONE KNOWS WHEN THEY LOSE THEIR MIND. BUT I'M SO LONELY!

(The music stops. LESLIE looks up. The BOY and GIRL exit to opposite sides. As if to a man standing over him)

I'm sorry. I just slipped and . . .

(Turning to the other side. There is a "man" there, too.)

Oh, thank you.

(Allowing the man to help him up, still with the sheet as a gown; softly to the man, intimately)

I'm sorry—I hate to trouble you, but I—I believe I've torn my gown. I seemed to have ripped . . . Oh, no, it can be repaired. Yes, I'm sure it can. But would you take me home now, please?

(There is a pause.)

Just take me home, please; take me home, please. Take me home now. Take me home. PLEASE TAKE ME HOME.

(The music now comes on and builds in a few seconds to top volume. LESLIE *screams above it. He drops the sheet, it falls down around him.)*

TAKE ME HOME, *SOMEONE!* TAKE ME HOME!

(The music stops. LESLIE *has run to the wall, to a far-off area, leaning against the wall. The Mozart is the only music remaining. Softly, whispering against the wall—to himself)*

Take me home. Take me home. Take me home. Take me home. Take me home. Take me home. Take me home. Take me home. Take me home. . . .

(The lights fade out slowly.)

THE END

THEATRE GENESIS

RALPH COOK, artistic director of Theatre Genesis.

Theatre Genesis, sponsored by St. Mark's Church in-the-Bouwerie, is a playwrights' workshop theatre. The concept, when Genesis began in August 1964, was to serve the playwright at that point in his career when he needs to be produced with maximum freedom and with continuity. In other words, we are not looking for plays to produce but writers who are at that point where they need a continuing relationship with a stage and actors in order to evolve. We feel there is a desperate need for the playwright to have a home in which to function without having continually to market himself in order to be produced.

At the heart of Genesis is the weekly workshop in which participating actors read scripts for the playwrights. A writer is invited to have a reading on the basis of submitted scripts which we feel show talent and ability. He may have several plays read before one is produced, if at all. Once produced, the playwright has priority in the workshop for the reading of new scripts, old scripts, works in progress, or for the improvisational use of the actors. The decision for production is made when a director connects with a play and both meet with the approval of the artistic director. Productions have a three-weekend run of twelve performances. If our produced writers are prolific and continue to use Genesis, we can serve only ten or twelve playwrights a year. However, the turnover is high; the best receive money offers and the worst feel unappreciated.

Genesis has presented thirty-three plays by seventeen writers. Beginning with Sam Shepard's *Cowboys* and *Rock Garden*, Theatre Genesis has defined itself in terms of a deeply subjective kind of realism and, within the Off-Off Broadway circuit, an almost conspicuous heterosexuality. Of our writers Shepard, Leonard Melfi, Murray Mednick, Tony Barsha, and Tom Sankey are most representative of the direction this theatre has taken.

The result of what we and the other theatres are doing is revolutionary. We are creating a truly indigenous theatre. The actors, directors, and writers are members of a geographical community and are presenting plays for members of that community, not as a special gala event, but as an integral everyday part of the life of the community. The audience, young and old, born of the streets of New York, or escapees from Ohio or Poland, come together to see themselves or their neighbors as they are, and perhaps to find the means of survival in this accelerated age.

Personally I have little hope for the survival of our civilization. But whatever hope we have lies with our artists, for they alone have the ability (if we do not continue to corrupt them) to withstand the onslaught of the mass media and the multitude of false gods. They alone have the ability to show us ourselves.

The time is late. Within this instantaneous electronic age the world is rapidly becoming one tribe, and the artist is assuming his original role of tribal actor and artificer. He gives us the existential now so that we can know, at least for a moment, who and where we are.

Here, now, in lower Manhattan the phenomenon is taking place: the beginning, the Genesis, of a cultural revolution. It is taking place out of utter necessity. Out of the necessity to survive. And yet everyone involved must find other means to support himself. An actor finds himself torn between accepting a role in a piece of Broadway entertainment or originating a role which defines not only himself but also his community. The playwright, if he is able to reach this audience, and is therefore of interest and profit to the commercial theatre, is then subjected to all the corrupting pressures of an already archaic economic structure.

I don't know how, within the existing structure, the means to subsidize this phenomenon can be found. I do know one thing: if we are to survive, it must be found.

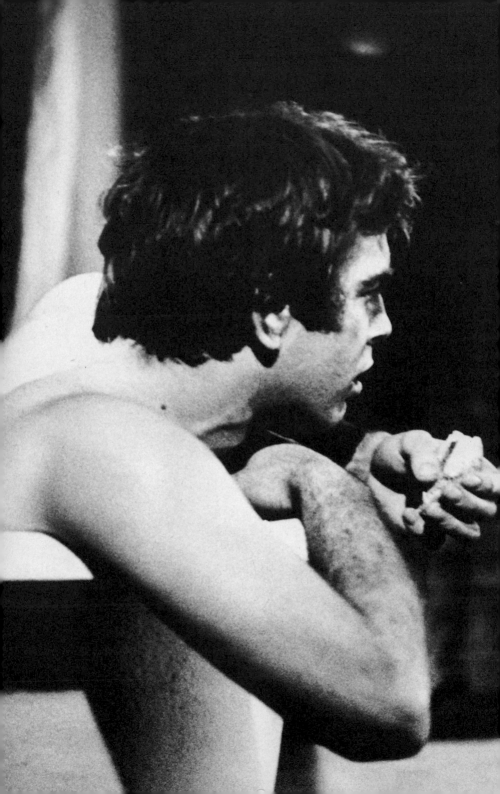

Chicago

by Sam Shepard

CHICAGO was first produced by Theatre Genesis at St. Mark's Church in-the-Bouwerie on Good Friday 1965. It was directed by Ralph Cook with the following cast:

POLICEMAN	Warren Finnerty
STU	Kevin O'Connor
JOY	Lyn Hutt
MYRA	Lenette Reuben
JOE	Paul Plummer
SALLY	Susanne English
JIM	Lee Kissman

SAM SHEPARD *was born in Fort Sheridan, Illinois, on November 5, 1943, and attended Mt. San Antonio College in California. From there he went across the country with the Bishop's Company Repertory Players, with whom he acted in* A Sleep of Prisoners *and other plays. He has had six plays produced Off-Off Broadway. Their titles are* Rock Garden, Cowboys, Dog, Rocking Chair, Chicago, *and* Icarus's Mother. *Off-Broadway, Theatre 1965 has produced his* Up to Thursday *as part of the New Playwrights' Series at the Cherry Lane Theatre.*

Chicago

by Sam Shepard

SCENE

(The lights dim down in the house. A POLICEMAN *comes out in front of the curtain with a club. He beats the curtain several times with the club, then walks into the audience and up the center aisle. He goes to the back of the house and bangs his club three times on the back of a chair. Someone reciting the "Gettysburg Address" comes on very loudly through the sound system. The curtains open. The lights come up slowly on a bare stage. Upstage center* STU *is sitting in a bathtub splashing water and talking in a singsong manner. The "Gettysburg Address" fades out as* STU *continues.)*

STU

And ya' walk through the town. With yer head on the ground. And ya' look all around through the town fer yer dog. Your dog Brown. He's yellow but ya' call him Brown anyhow. And sit in the hay. And ya' say. What a day. This is it. It's the day that ya' say is okay. Anyway. Anyhow. You know by now. That yer dog is dead and ya' don't care anyhow. 'Cause ya' didn't really like him in the first place. So ya' say. What a day. In the hay. Anyway. And ya' walk through the town and around. Then ya' see another tree. And ya' pee on the ground. 'Cause it's nice and ya' don't think twice. Ya' just do and it's done. And it's fun. Ho, ho.

JOY
(Off right)
Biscuits!

STU

Biscuits in the sun. And ya' run. And it's fun. Ya' have a gun. It's yer own. Ya' don't care. You can even shoot a bear. If ya' have any hair. If ya' don't. Ya' don't. If ya' do. It's true. And yer through anywho.

JOY
(Off right)
Biscuits are ready!

STU

Teddy and Freddy and all the stupid people having fun with a gun. And ya' run all around. Through the town. What a way. To spend a day. In the hay. By the way. It's okay. Stay away.
(JOY comes on from right in a bathrobe, she yells at STU.)

JOY
Biscuits! Biscuits! Come on!
(She goes off right. STU stands suddenly in the bathtub; he is wearing long pants and tennis shoes without a shirt.)

STU
Just a second! Just a second!
(JOY comes back on from right.)

JOY
What?

STU
A towel.

JOY
Just a second.
(She goes off right.)

STU

If it was warm I could go without a towel. Seeing as how it's cold, I'll need one.

100

(JOY *comes back on with a towel; she throws it at* STU, *then goes back off right.* STU *stays standing up in the tub drying himself.*)
Thanks.

JOY
(*Off right*)
Okay.

STU
I meant if the sun were out. That kind of warmth. Not just warm but a sun kind of warmth. You know? Like the beach.

JOY
(*Off right*)
The beach has sun.

STU
I know. You just lie there and the sun dries you and the sand gets all stuck to you. It sticks all over. In your toes. In your ears. Up your crotch. Aaah! Sand between your legs! Aaah! Sticking in your pores. Goddamn!
(*He sits back down in the tub and puts the towel over his head; he talks like an old lady, using the towel as a bandanna.*)
All you young little girlies out there paradin' around in yer flimsies. Make me all ashamed and pink in the face to think a' that.

JOY
(*Off right*)
What?

STU
Two-pieces and one-pieces and bare-chested things going on. No upbringin'. That's it. That's where it comes from. A

101

lack a' concern on the part a' the parents and all. Flimsy morality. Dirty shame.

(JOY *comes on fast from right.*)

JOY

Cold biscuits! Do you dig cold biscuits? The butter's cold, too. The jam's cold. I hope you're glad.

(*She goes off right.* STU *stands again with the towel still draped over his head; he talks like an old lady.*)

STU

Looky here, missy. Don't be so high and mighty and flashy, all of a sudden. Just 'cause ya' got big boobies. Thank the Lord fer that. But that happens to be a gift. Ya' were bestowed with that chest a' yours. And don't forget it. Praise the Lord!

JOY
(Off right)
Fuck off!

(STU *takes the towel off his head and starts drying himself again; he talks in a normal voice.*)

STU

Biscuits. Who needs biscuits at this hour? Who ever needs biscuits? Joy?

JOY
(Off right)
What?

STU

Who needs biscuits?

JOY

Peasants in Mexico.

STU

Peasants make their own. Biscuits were invented to trick

people into believing they're really eating food! They aren't
any good at all. They're just dough. A hunk of dough that
goes down and makes a gooey ball in your stomach. It makes
you feel full. Biscuits are shit!

(JOY *throws a bunch of biscuits from off right; they hit* STU
in the head, STU *picks one up and takes a bite out of it, he
sits back down in the tub and continues eating the biscuit;
a phone rings off left,* JOY *crosses the stage and exits left
still wearing the nightgown, she answers the phone, she
talks off left.*)

JOY
Hello. Hi. Oh, you're kidding. Is that right? Oh Myra. Well
when's he leaving? He left? He's gone? You do? Oh fine.
Yes. I got the job. Yes, it's final. Well they called last night.
Last night. Uh-huh. Two weeks. A week maybe. The sooner
the better. I'll see. Well I have a few things to do. Yes. Okay.
'Bye.

(*She hangs up; she comes on from left dressed in a bra and
slip, she crosses the stage.*)
How's your biscuit?

STU
Good. How's yours?
(*She exits right.*)

JOY
(*Off right*)
Myra's coming.

STU
Did you say you got the job? Did I hear you say that?

JOY
I said Myra's coming.

103

STU

On the phone. Did you say you got the job?

JOY

Yes.
(STU *stands suddenly in the tub and starts yelling.*)

STU

You did not!

JOY
(*Off right*)

Yes!

STU

They hired you!

JOY

Yes!

STU

Good! I'm really glad!

JOY

Good!

STU

I'm really, really glad. When are you going?
(JOY *comes on from right brushing her hair and still wearing the bra and slip.*)

JOY

Oh I don't know.

STU

You don't?

JOY

Soon.

STU
Good.
(JOY *climbs into the tub with* STU.)
Don't! You can't get in here.

JOY
How come?

STU
Because there's not enough water.

JOY
Don't be stupid. We can fill it up.

STU
It'll overflow.

JOY
Myra's coming.

STU
You told me.
(JOY *kisses* STU; *they embrace for a while, then sit in the tub facing each other;* JOY *brushes her hair.*)

JOY
It's really nice out here.

STU
Out where?

JOY
On the water.

STU
(*Putting the towel on his head and talking like an old lady.*)
All you young things are the same. Corny. Corny young girls. That's what.

JOY

I love the water.

STU

Ya' all love the water. Water in the nighttime. With the moon hangin' over yer filthy little head.

JOY

It's so quiet.

STU

Yeah. Ya' like the quiet 'cause ya' don't take the time to listen when it's not quiet.

JOY

Listen to the waves.

STU

Listen yerself, missy. I heard water slappin' on the pier before. I got ears.

JOY

I could stay here forever. Feel the breeze.

STU

A corny young virgin. That's what.

JOY

It's so nice.
(*She leans over the side of the tub as though it were a boat.*)

STU

Nice, nice. No nicer than most things.

JOY

Look at the fish.
(STU *leans over and looks.*)

STU

Them's barracuda, lady. They eat people when they feel like it.

JOY

They wouldn't eat me.

STU

They'd eat you like nobody's business.

JOY

They're really big.

STU

Big as they come.
(MYRA *comes on from left dressed in a fur coat and dark glasses and carrying a suitcase. She stands looking on.*)

JOY

That's awful.

STU

See the way they flash around. That's 'cause they're hungry.

JOY

Really?

STU

Starvin' to death.

JOY

Damn.

STU

Just lookin' fer a nice young virgin.

JOY

They don't eat people.

STU

Just lookin' fer somethin' to bite.
(*He grabs her and tries to push her out of the tub.*)

JOY

Stop it!

STU

All them fishies gettin' ready fer a feast.

JOY

Cut it out!
(They stand struggling with each other.)

STU

Big striped fishes with long teeth and pink tongues.

JOY

Stop!

STU
(Normal voice)
They like you. They want you for their very own. They want to eat you up!

JOY

No!
(They kiss for a while.)

STU

Myra's here.

MYRA

Hello, Joy. Are you ready?

JOY

No.

STU

She's ready.

JOY

I am not.

STU

She got hired.
(JOY climbs out of the tub and starts brushing her hair.)

MYRA

It's a good job.

JOY

It's all right.

(JOY exits right brushing her hair, MYRA follows behind her, they go off. STU stands looking down at the floor.)

STU

Tough luck, fish. You're really ugly anyway. Eat some little fish. Minnows or something. Seaweed. Try some seaweed for a change. You're going to be in bad shape if you keep going around like that. In schools. In all that crappy black water. Bumping your dumb heads into rocks and boulders and making your tongues bleed. Stupid. Swim. Go ahead. Let me see you. Don't just hang there treading water.

(He kneels down in the tub looking over the edge.)

What's wrong? I see you, stupid. Go down. Dive or something. Beat it! All right! Stay there. See if I care.

(He lies back in the tub and puts his feet up on the edge.)

You can't wait forever. You'll have to go when it gets dark. People will start looking for you when it gets dark. They'll be out in boats. They'll have long hip boots on and pipes and mosquito juice on their faces. They'll have bottles full of worms and poles for you. They'll get in all their little boats and push them out in the water. Then they'll whisper to each other about what a nice night it is and how still it is and look at all the fireflies. Then they'll row very softly out to the middle. Out in the deep part. And they'll break out their thermos bottles full of coffee and split pea soup. And they'll drink and whisper about you. About how big you are and how striped you are and how nice it would be to have your head cut off and mounted over the fireplace. They'll get out their poles and the worms and the hooks and drop them over the side. The worm will just float for a while, then he'll have a little spasm and wriggle on the hook. Then he'll drown and sink all the way to the bottom and die in front of your long noses. You'll watch him for a while, see. Then you'll move a little bit. You're pretty hungry but you're not sure. So you take your time. You're down there moving slowly around this worm, taking your time. And they're up there drinking split pea soup and grinning and pointing at the moon and the pier and all the trees. You're both hung up.

(The phone rings off left, JOY *crosses the stage and exits left,* STU *remains standing and looking off left.)*

JOY
(Off left)
Hello. How are you, Joe? Sure. Okay. Yes, I got the job. Of course. How about you? Well, pretty soon I guess. Yes I bought my ticket. Uh-huh. Well as soon as I can. Yes. Sure. Come on over. Okay. Good. 'Bye.

(She hangs up and comes on from left carrying a fishing pole, she crosses to STU *and kisses him on the stomach then exits right.)*

STU
That was Joe huh?
(He sits.)

JOY
(Off right)
Yes. He's coming over.

STU
Good.

MYRA
(Off right)
Good biscuits, Joy.

JOY

They're all right.

STU

Are you packing, Joy?

JOY

What?

STU

Are you getting your stuff ready?

JOY

Yes.

STU

That's going to be a good trip.

JOY

I guess so.

STU

All that way on a train. The seats fold back so you can sleep if you want to. You can look out the window too. You can see all kinds of different houses and people walking around.
(JOE *comes on from left wearing a suit and dark glasses and carrying a fishing pole and a suitcase; he looks at* STU *for a while, then crosses the stage and exits right.*)
They have one whole car where you eat. And another car just for drinking. The tables are nailed to the floor so they don't jiggle. You can buy a whole dinner for about five bucks. They even give you a full pitcher of ice water. They just leave it on the table so you don't have to keep asking for water. And a silver cup full of toothpicks. You sit there and pick your teeth and look out the window. Then you have to leave. They force you to leave because there's a whole line of people waiting to eat. They're all hungry.

111

JOY
(Off right)
Hi, Joe.

JOE
(Off right)
Hi.

MYRA
(Off right)
Have a biscuit.

JOE
Thanks.

STU
They stop once in a while but you can only get off at the big stations. You can only get off at places like St. Louis or Cincinnati. None of the small towns. And your butt aches after a while. Your butt really starts to ache. You can hardly stand it. So you have to get up and walk around. Up and down the aisles. Back and forth.

JOE
(Off right)
Hm. Real butter.

JOY
(Off right)
Yes. It's starting to melt though.

STU
Your butt aches so bad that your legs even start to ache. Your legs can fall asleep on a train. Then your feet. You have to walk fast. It's better to sit in the rest room because you can stretch. You can stretch your legs out in there. And there's old men in there taking nips on little

wine bottles. They get drunk in there and throw up on the floor. Their wives don't even know it because they're asleep in the folding chairs.

MYRA
(Off right)
Delicious.

JOE
(Off right)
Good jam, too.

STU
Then everyone falls asleep. Almost everyone at once. It's dark so they figure they have to I guess. The porter turns the lights out and right away everyone's asleep. There's a little girl running up and down the aisle. She doesn't make any noise because everyone's sleeping. There's a Marine making it with somebody's wife because her husband's drunk in the rest room. There's a cowboy picking his teeth and spitting little gobs of food into the aisle. Some fat guy is farting and he doesn't even know it. The smell drifts down the aisle and stinks up the whole car. One fart after another. Big windy farts that sort of make a whizzing sound. Nobody can hear him but it stinks the whole car up.
(SALLY enters from left wearing dark glasses, fur coat, and carrying a suitcase and a fishing pole; she watches STU for a while, then crosses to the tub and stands there.)
He moves a little in the seat because he can feel it I guess. His wife moves a little and rubs her nose. Then they keep on sleeping. The car stinks more and more. The smell gets into the seats and the pillows and the rug. Everyone's smelling it at the same time. They sleep more and more. Then it's morning.

SALLY

Hi.

STU
(Sitting up and yawning)
Whew! What time is it?

SALLY

Seven.

STU

Are you going too?

SALLY

Yep.

STU

Do you have all your stuff?

SALLY

Yep.

STU

It's a good day to leave.

SALLY

Why?

STU

I mean it's sunny. The sun's out.

SALLY

It's cold though.

STU

But when the sun's out you don't notice it.

SALLY

I guess. I'm going to eat.

114

STU
Okay.
(She exits right.)
The water's up. The sun's on the water already.
(He stands and yells off right.)
Hey, everybody! The sun's on the water!

MYRA
(Off right)
Really?

STU
Yeah. And the tide's up. We should take a swim.

JOY
(Off right)
It's too early.
(STU puts the towel over his head.)

STU
(Talking like an old lady)
Dainty little things. Too early. Too early to swim. Water's
too cold. There's a little bitty wind skippin' over the sand.
The shells are too sharp for them dainty feet. Tsk, tsk. Got
to wear your tennies on account of the shells.
*(JIM comes on from left wearing a suit and dark glasses and
carrying a suitcase and fishing pole; he watches STU.)*
Got to wear a shirty on account of the sun. Can't lay around
in the sand on account of your crotch. Smear a lot a' chicken
fat on yer tiny fragile legs. Get back in the cabin, girlie!
Don't go faintin' on the beach!

JIM
Are you going, Stu?

STU
(Still old lady)

None a' yer business, sonny! Get away from this beach! Go
on! Get off my sand! Get away from the shells! Git! Git!

JIM
Hey Stu.
(He gives STU *the finger and goes off right.)*

STU
That don't shock me, sonny! I been around. That kind a'
smut don't bother no one nowadays. This is the twentieth
century, buddy!

MYRA
(Off right)
Hi, Jim.

JIM
(Off right)
Hi.

JOY
Are you ready?

JIM
Sure.

STU
You ain't gonna bother nobody nowadays. You're a bunch
a' sissies! A bunch a' pantywaists! Nobody cares about the
likes a' you! No moxy! No spunk! Can't even swim on account a' the smoke ya' put in your lungs. A bunch a' fatsoes.
A bunch a' faggots prancin' around. Dancin' in the streets
with yer make-up on. Swishin' into yer gay restaurants! No
balls! That's what! No hair on yer chest!

JOE
(Off right)
Do you have everything?

MYRA
(Off right)
I think so.

JIM
Tooth paste?

JOY
Yep.

STU
(Still old lady)
Anyway the water's up. There won't be a boat for days.
They don't come in when it's high like this. The tide and
all. Boats are chicken too. Chickens run boats. A bunch a'
cowards. They'll wait for it to calm. It'll warm up and
they'll come in with their sails down and their nets hangin'
over the edge. They'll all be drinkin' gin and singin' sea
songs. They'll all be horny for the young virgins that walk
the beaches in their two-piece flimsy things. Then they'll
come onto the land and start screwing everything in sight.
The boats'll be hung up for days because everybody's screwing on the beach. They'll like it more and more. Once they
get the taste for it they won't stop. The boats will be there
for months because everybody's screwing. Nobody wants to
go nowhere because screwing is all they need. Screwing and
screwing. And all those boats just sitting out there with
their sails down and their nets hanging and rotting in the
sun. Years go by and they're still screwing. Old sailors with
bald heads and old virgins with gray hair. The whole beach
littered with bodies on top of each other. The boats are
sinking! All those rotten boats falling into the ocean. One
at a time. They break into bits and crack each other as they
go down. One at a time. They sink. Pieces of wood float
and wash up onto the beach but nobody cares. Nobody

needs boats or wood or sails or nets. There's a whole new crop of corny virgins walking around. Up and down the beach in their two-pieces. Nobody stops. More babies from the virgins. Males and females up and down the beach. No clothes any more. A mound of greasy bodies rolling in sperm and sand sticking to their backs and sand in their hair. Hair growing all over. Down to their feet. Pubic hair without bows or ribbons.

(He talks in normal voice and takes the towel off his head.) Hair on their toes. Fires! Fires at night. All over the island there's huge fires flaring and they all lie around. They lie there fucking by the fire and picking each other's nose. They lick each other's arms and growl and purr and fart all they want to. They roll around farting and spitting and licking up and down. Long tongues and wet legs. Then they build a house. A big house way up on the side of a hill. It takes a year to build. It's one house with one room and a fire pit in the middle. They all go in and sit on the floor and make rugs. They make rugs because the floor is cold and they don't like the cold. They start weaving and sewing. Big huge heavy rugs with fringe around the edge and diamond shapes in the middle. Orange and red rugs with yellow diamonds. They stop screwing, see, and they just make rugs. All day. Years of making rugs until the whole house is covered. The walls are covered and the ceiling and the floor. The windows are blocked up and they sit. The fire's out because of the rugs. It's warm. They're very warm inside. Sitting. It's dark, see. Pitch black and no sound. Because of the rugs. Then they start to giggle. One of them starts and they all start. One after another until they can't stop. The whole house is giggling. Then they scream, see. They start screaming all together because they can't breathe. On account of the rugs. The rugs are all sewn together and it's very warm. It's boiling hot inside. They start

to sweat and run around. They bump into each other because it's dark. They can't see so they hit and claw each other with their nails. They have long nails. They kick and scream and the sweat is rolling off them. They can't breathe and it's hot. They're screaming, see.

(*Off stage right the actors giggle,* STU *sits slowly in the bathtub, the giggling stops.*)

And they come out. One at a time. They walk in a line out of the house. One behind the other. Down the side of the hill. Through the woods. They don't say anything. They don't even breathe. They just walk in a line. Down to the beach. They walk across the beach and right into the water. One behind the other. They just keep walking until you can't see them any more.

(*He lies back in the tub so that his head is out of view and his feet hang over the edge.* JOY *comes on from right dressed in a bright red hat and a red dress; she is pulling a wagon loaded with all the suitcases. The rest of the actors come on whistling and cheering, they all hold their fishing poles, they stand in a group stage right waving and throwing kisses at* JOY *as* JOY *backs up slowly with the wagon waving back to them.*)

MYRA

Have a good time!

SALLY

So long, Joy!

JOE

So long!

JIM

Good luck out there!

JOE

See you, babe!

JIM
'Bye!

JOE
'Bye, 'bye!

JOY
'Bye!

MYRA
Say hello for me!

JOE
Don't forget!

JIM
Have fun!

JOE
Good luck!

JOY
Thanks!

JOE
See you later!

(JOY *keeps backing up with the wagon and exits left. The four actors throw kisses, then walk slowly downstage; they stand in a line across the stage facing the audience, then they all cast their lines into the audience. They sit simultaneously and look at the audience while holding their poles.*)

STU

(With his head still unseen)

Then the water goes out again because it's nighttime. I guess it goes out. Yes. At night the water always goes out. And the sand gets all dry in the place where the water used to be. You can hear it making little slapping sounds and getting farther away from the pier. There's a breeze sort of.

One of those high breezes that just hits the top of your head and blows paper cups down the beach. Your back shivers a little and you get goose bumps on your legs. Your toes start to sweat. The sweat runs down between your toes and your feet swell up and stick to your socks. You can't move because your feet are stuck. You can't move your head. Your head stays straight and your eyes are wide open. You can't blink your eyes. Your hands sweat just like your feet. Your fingers swell up like your toes.

(The lights start to dim slowly.)

The sweat runs down your arms and down your legs. You're looking out and you can see the water. You can see it in the dark because it's white. Like milk. The whole top is covered with milk. It smells. Your nose is burning from the smell but you can't move. You keep looking to the other side. The smell gets worse and your ears start to hum. You can see these little dots on the other side. These lights. Your eyes stay open. Then you move. You start to move slowly up the beach. Your feet hurt and your nose is bleeding from the smell. Then you see the lights again. And they blink. One after the other. Between the trees. You can see them blinking. On and off. A whole town.

(JOY backs on stage from left again pulling the wagon; she exits right.)

Your eyes start blinking with the lights. Your feet start moving. You can feel them move inside your socks. Then your arms. You're running. You can feel the breathing. Panting sort of. The wind comes in through your nose and dries the blood. You can taste it. Your mouth opens and the wind comes in. Your body's moving. The sweat dries on your legs and the wind hits you. You're going now. Much faster and the breathing gets harder. You can see the lights better now. Yellow lights between the trees. The smell stops. The humming stops. The lights go out.

121

(The lights come up to their full brightness, STU *jumps out of the bathtub and crosses very fast downstage center facing the audience, the other actors remain sitting and staring at the audience.)*

STU

Good!

(He breathes in and out very fast.)

That's great! See my stomach. In and out. It's breathing. I'm taking it in. The air. What a fine bunch of air I'm taking in. Now I'm taking it in through my nose. See.

(He breathes through his nose.)

Aaah! Great! Now my mouth.

(He breathes through his mouth.)

Good! In and out! Ladies and gentlemen, the air is fine! All this neat air gathered before us! It's too much!

(The other actors start to breathe slowly, gradually, making sounds as they inhale and exhale.)

The place is teeming with air. All you do is breathe. Easy. One, two. One, two. In. Out. Out, in. I learned this in fourth grade. Breathing, ladies and gentlemen! Before your very eyes. Outstanding air. All you need to last a day. Two days. A week. Month after month of breathing until you can't stop. Once you get the taste of it. The hang of it. What a gas. In your mouth and out your nose. Ladies and gentlemen, it's fantastic!

(They all breathe in unison as JOY *backs on stage from right pulling the wagon; she exits slowly left as the lights dim and go out. There are three loud knocks from the back of the house.)*

THE END

THE JUDSON POETS' THEATRE

REV. AL CARMINES, assistant minister and head of the arts program at Judson Memorial Church.

The Judson Poets' Theatre is the result of two concerns of Judson Memorial Church. The congregation of this church believes and acts on the premise that the purpose of the church in our time is to serve the needs of the community. One need in our community was for a space where new playwrights could be produced free from certain commercial pressures and popular taste. Another concern was for the church itself, that it might be exposed to the work of these playwrights and thus hear the secular prophets in our city. Both of these concerns created a theatre that has experienced wide variety but also kept a kind of consistency through five years of producing plays. The variety is a result of the freedom which the church has allowed and indeed encouraged in its theatre; the consistency has resulted from a freedom within the church and the constant response of a community which for various reasons is associated with Judson.

Judson is primarily a playwright's theatre. The work itself has been the center of attention and effort. Every theoretical problem of acting and staging is met, but within the context of a particular production. Each production develops in the style of the director and cast; there is a kind of community that develops around each production and thus in the theatre itself. A complex of the same directors working with different actors and the same actors working with different directors creates an exciting experience for all.

We do not subscribe to the idea that a theatre of intimacy and experimentation must mean a calculated shoddiness in production. We place a premium on "clean" and skilled presentations and we have been fortunate in having good and talented technical help. There has been much concentration on the problem of style; the director is often the central fulcrum of the creative event here. Because there is also at the church a Judson Art Gallery and a Judson Dance Theatre, there has been a most fruitful and important cross-fertilization of work in the theatre between art, dance, happenings, and drama. Some of our most interesting work in the theatre has resulted from this collaboration. The space itself has been shaped and "bent" in various ways to fulfill each playwright and director's desires.

We are not concerned with messages or views of theatre which would intrinsically relate it to the church. Nor are we concerned with a particular theory of theatre. We do want to do good plays well—and that is almost all that can be said about our purpose. At one time I saw the Off-Off Broadway movement including our own theatre as the stepping stone to bigger and better theatre (Broadway, Off-Broadway). I no longer feel that way. I think that *the most important* theatre in New York is in churches and coffee shops and lofts. Commercial theatre is lost because it is controlled by men who distrust and are condescending to the public. Perhaps here is a connection with the church after all—for we believe in people enough to give the best theatre we can.

Our problems at Judson are the same as those of any Off-Off Broadway theatre—how to keep from being "cliquish"—how to keep focusing on the work rather than ourselves—how to keep from being dominated by audience or critics—and, of course, how to do a lot on a very little bit of money. But believing in people, we also believe in the validity of the theatrical event—and that's what keeps us going.

The Great American Desert

by Joel Oppenheimer

THE GREAT AMERICAN DESERT, directed by Lawrence Korn-feld, premièred at the Judson Poets' Theatre, November 18, 1961. It had the following cast:

THE OLD COWBOY	Gil Henderson
THE GUNNY	Jerome Raphel
THE YOUNG COWBOY	Ray Girardin
THE WHORE	C. Cornelia
THE BANKER'S BEAUTIFUL DAUGHTER	Joyce Glassman
THE BANKER	John Marshall
THE SHERIFF	Laurence Hellenberg
THE MADAM	Otis Burger
WYATT EARP	Jack Wesley
WILD BILL HICKOK	Anthony Hilliard
BILLY THE KID	Marty Washburn
DOC HOLLIDAY	Paul Blackburn

JOEL OPPENHEIMER *was born in 1930 in Yonkers, New York. He attended public schools in Yonkers and studied at Cornell University, the University of Chicago, and Black Mountain College. He has published two books of poetry. Grove Press will publish a book of his plays, including* The Great American Desert *and* Like a Hill. *His other works include* The Dutiful Son *and* The Love Bit, *and he is published in many current literary magazines and several poetry anthologies.*

The Great American Desert

by Joel Oppenheimer

SCENE

(All the action takes place somewhere west of Laramie; the time of the play is sunup in the morning to sundown at night. The play was presented in three-quarter round, with an additional stage area ("heaven") on which the four heavenly heroes sit. It is covered at the front enough to conceal their legs and waists as they sit. BILLY THE KID *sits farthest from the ladder by which they ascend, in a slightly separated area, in this case a wider, lower platform.*

Very low lights come up on stage and hold, while the lights on heaven begin slowly to build. The four heavenly heroes enter upstage left and move diversely across the main stage area, heading generally toward the ladder leading to heaven. They maintain the order necessary for their seating in heaven: BILLY THE KID *first; he is dressed in rough range, or even farm clothes, and he carries a rifle.* DOC HOLLIDAY *next; he is dressed in black, but fastidiously, though not foppishly.* WYATT EARP *next; he is dressed neatly, with almost a hint of the puritan about him; he has a pistol which is holstered and tied to his leg.* WILD BILL HICKOK *last; he, of course, has shoulder-length hair and a pointed beard; he is dressed as foppishly as possible, ruffled shirt, etc., and his gun is tucked in his waistband. As they walk they hum, in unison, "Wagonwheels." The humming continues as they reach the ladder and begin the climb to heaven; it will stop when the tune reaches a natural stopping point. Once in heaven they*

129

begin to take their seats. WYATT *reminds* DOC *about* BILLY'S
rifle. BILLY *surrenders his rifle to* DOC *after a token protest,
and* DOC *then leans it back against the wall between* WYATT
and himself. When all four are comfortable in their seats,
WYATT *nods to the stage manager, the lights begin to build
on stage and revert to their normal holding position on
heaven. The three* COWBOYS *are discovered downstage left,
sleeping.)*

OLD COWBOY

Goddamn! Morning!
*(He stretches, crawls out of bedroll, dresses, kicks each of the
other two, and exits upstage right.)*

GUNNY

Now what in the good hell he have to do that for?
(He begins dressing.)
There are goddamn easier ways wakin' a man up. And you,
goddamn you—get up, you lazy bastard, it's morning! The
dew's on the frost, and goddamn, you know . . .

YOUNG COWBOY

The sun ain't nowhere near full up, and you both of you
raisin' all kinds of hell. We only got another day to ride in,
is all, we ain't doin' nothin'.
(He is still stretched flat.)

GUNNY

Yeah, but we still got to do it. Come on now, get yourself
up, before he's back and screamin' again. He's probably
takin' care of the horses, so I'll get you some firewood and
start this up again. You move your ass and get that goddamn
breakfast goin'. I'm hungry.
(Exits upstage right.)

YOUNG COWBOY

Hungry. He's hungry. The two of them is always hungry.
I might as well goddamn be married to the two of them.

And always I got to do the cookin'. Though, God knows, I ain't about to eat anythin' either of them cooks. Probably poison a rattler, anything either of them cooks.

(Starts getting breakfast materials from his saddlebag.)

OLD COWBOY

(Re-enters)

Them goddamn horses ain't holdin' up so well. Two, three more days of this, they're gone. We better either be out of it by then, or hope we find someone to buy some new ones off'n, even a Indian.

YOUNG COWBOY

You ain't buyin' no goddamned Indian ponies with my share of that money. I'd a heap rather walk first, even into Albuquerque, and that's three hundred miles away.

OLD COWBOY

You sayin' it, boy, but you ain't about to do it. You be, as a matter of fact you be the first one to start cryin' if we have to walk. Listen, I took us through this far, I take us out, and you better believe it.

GUNNY

(Re-enters with firewood)

Here's your firewood. You goin' to get the water, or I have to do that too? Damn I'm hungry.

YOUNG COWBOY

There's no call at all for you to be pushin' it that way, breakfast goin' to get here, never fear. Besides, you bein' such a big desperado, I think it's only fittin' you get the water, you so big and strong and desperate for it.

GUNNY

Damn this fuckin desert anyhow. All this sweat over water, goddamn when I was a boy back home in Illinois they used to talk about the plains. . . . I thought to myself like the garden of Eden. Now we here, fightin' from one stinkin' waterhole to the next, nothin' but sand and bushes in betwixt.

(Exits upstage right with bucket. As he leaves stage area, BLACKOUT on stage, LIGHTS UP on heaven. This will be standard procedure for all readings of commercials. They are to be read by individual heavenly heroes in random sequence. Each commercial is read from a typed card in either a straight speaking voice or standard—radio or television—English, or perhaps a pedantic lecturer's voice. The voice used must not be that of the heavenly hero in character.)

COMMERCIAL: THE GREAT AMERICAN DESERT

In the early days of the west the Great American Desert was the favorite hiding place of many desperate men, and for good reason. This desolate stretch of land, called by some "the great plains," stretches across the western heart of America. It is not only hard to traverse, but also, due probably to the intense dryness and sundry allied atmospheric factors, seems to have affected not only the hearts and souls of the men who moved on it, but their very destinies also, and, indeed, that of America itself.

(During the commercial, while stage is blacked out, the OLD COWBOY and the YOUNG COWBOY move from their position downstage left to upstage right, assuming the same relative positions, while the GUNNY recrosses stage to downstage left, so that he may re-enter to correspond with the change. Think of the move, and the following ones, as being a different camera angle on the same scene.)

OLD COWBOY

You talk about desperadoes and you kiddin' about it, but that's just about what it comes to. If we weren't so fuckin desperate for a hidin' place it wouldn't be so bad. But we here on this fuckin desert, and nothin' goin' to get us out but guts. And I got those, even if you two boys don't. I'm goin' to come out of this.

GUNNY

(Re-enters with bucket)

What you talkin' about? We all goin' to make it. Hear? Here's your water. You forgettin' who you travelin' with.
(He turns his back on the other two and begins fooling with his gun, trying his draw, checking the loads and the action.)

OLD COWBOY

I ain't about to forget anything, and most of all I ain't forgettin' how the three of us have rid together three years, come hell or high water. But after three years I know you, and I know him, and most of all, I know me. You the best damn gun around, only because you don't care a doodly squat for you or me or him or anybody alive. And he, once trouble start, he goin' to do his job better'n any man alive, because he care too damn much about everything. And I goin' to keep on bein' the leader, the damn boss man, because the only thing I care about at all is gettin' the three of us out of whatever we got into for whatever damn reason we picked to get into it. And that's all.

GUNNY

Trouble with you is, you got it all figured out. But I don't give no goddamn, long as I'm gettin' mine.

YOUNG COWBOY

Balls! There go the bucket. Watch the fire, will you, while I get me more water. It's just startin' to lay nice for cookin'.
(Exits downstage left.)

GUNNY

Man, he make such a big deal about cookin' I could die

here of hunger. The fire got to lay just right, and if he don't like the way something taste he throw it out.

> YOUNG COWBOY
> *(Re-enters)*

Listen, don't you worry, hear? You goin' to get your breakfast, coffee, bacon, and you treat me right, shut that fat mouth you got, might even fry some beans in the bargain.

> *(Aside to* OLD COWBOY*)*

Seen sign of Arikara down to the waterhole. They must've been here last night whilst we was sleepin'.

> GUNNY
> *(He is working with his gun again.)*

What in hell's all the whisperin' for? I got the fire goin', I got my bedroll done up, the horses is waitin', all ready to go, and damn! I'm ready to go too, except I ain't got any fuckin breakfast to keep my belly warm whilst I ride.

> OLD COWBOY
> *(Aside to* YOUNG COWBOY*)*

I seen it too, out by the horses, but I figure they don't mean no harm, or they would have done it already.

> *(Aloud)*

Listen, the boy's got a while to go there, so cool down. Anyhow, you know you goin' to get your bellyful some day, and I don't necessarily mean breakfast either.

> GUNNY

You so goddamn funny it hurts.

> YOUNG COWBOY

Okay, boys, breakfast be ready in one shake, and I don't mean maybe. You boys ought to know better. I been here not so long, but I plan to be here a long time more. Only way I'm going to do that is keep eatin' steady. So don't you worry none about your food.

COMMERCIAL: FOOD, THE STAPLE OF HUMAN BEINGS
Food has always been an integral part of all human, and indeed animal life, as far as is known. Evidences of what are thought to have been food dishes have been found in the middens of the earliest of peoples. Especially in an alien environment such as the Great American Desert was food important, and particularly a good breakfast. A good breakfast, remember, is a healthy breakfast.

(During the commercial the three COWBOYS *have moved upstage left. They are seated, eating.)*

GUNNY

Man, this what I been waitin' for. Only thing missin' is those beans you was talkin' about. I could sure use some beans along about now.

OLD COWBOY

The beans'll come, boy. Right now fill your belly on what you got. Life is too short. I remember being in Sonora once, outside the town of Sonora on that goddamned Mexican desert. Ate nothin' but cacti for five days, and damn glad, too. I came through, boy, I lived. And that was 'cause I wanted to, and wasn't worryin' about no beans or nothin'.

GUNNY

Man, all I said was, I wanted some beans, some goddamn beans.

YOUNG COWBOY

All right, goddamnit, they're coming. You think I just goin' to throw beans at you boys? First I got to add a little salt and pepper and chili powder which I got here in my saddlebags; I got to throw in a little ketchup, which it breaks my heart 'cause I ain't got any to throw in, but leastwise

I got to give that good chili powder half a chance to settle in amongst the goddamn beans afore I throw them at you.

GUNNY

Man, I was just talking, is all. All the time a big goddamn fuss, every time I open up my mouth.
(*The beans are dished out.*)

OLD COWBOY

Wouldn't be a bad idea, boys, to check your guns. We run so hard out of that town, and what with the sand and all, God knows what happen to them.
(*He exchanges a meaningful glance with the* YOUNG COWBOY.)

GUNNY

You right, man. I'm goin' to check mine again right now. Couldn't do without little Samuel here.

COMMERCIAL: THE SIX GUN WON THE WEST

While it is true that barbed wire was a contributory factor to the winning of the West, and, indeed, one of utmost importance, we must consider Samuel Colt's six gun, or revolver, as the crucial development in this direction. Without the six gun, which, as you probably know, could fire six shots in quick succession, without reloading, to aid the frontiersman, the Indians, possessors of the finest light cavalry in the world, would, no doubt, have beaten off these earlier venturers into the western vastnesses.

(*The three* COWBOYS *have moved to downstage right. The* YOUNG COWBOY *is standing practicing his draw.*)

GUNNY

You aimin' to shoot a snake? Bring it up, sonny, you'll lose a toe.

136

YOUNG COWBOY

Thanks.

(Puts gun away)

Sure can't wait till we hit a town. Sure am gettin' hungry for somethin' besides bacon, beans, and coffee, even if I do know how to cook 'em all.

GUNNY

Laddybuck, I hope you don't mean things like steak and such. I sure hope you ain't talkin' about things like that, all that talk of bein' hungry.

YOUNG COWBOY

Sheeit! What you take me for? A little dewy-eyed boy? Course I ain't talkin' about things like steak. I talkin' about pussy

(WHORE enters upstage right and crosses to upstage center. She sits, back to audience, as if in front of a mirror.)

some good old couze, even just a little old bit. I get away from it two, three days, especially with a bunch of old goats like you two, I miss it more than when I been out on roundup, or in the hills for maybe six months. The more I get it, the more I want it, seems.

OLD COWBOY

Yeah boy. You young ones, you cause all the goddamn trouble in this world. You hadna been foolin' round that banker's daughter

(The BANKER'S BEAUTIFUL DAUGHTER enters downstage left and crosses to downstage left edge of platform, where she sits writing in her diary.)

we still been workin' on the Double-O right now, and just wakin' us up out of nice soft bunkbeds, and eatin' oatmeal for breakfast, with some ham 'n' eggs.

137

GUNNY

Yeah, you sayin' that, but you forgettin' we wouldn' have no seven thousand dollars in our saddlebags right now, hadn't the little one been playin' round. Boy, you can go on like that any ole time, if it keeps gettin' us this kind of money.

(BANKER and SHERIFF enter upstage right and stand with back to audience as if at a bar.)

YOUNG COWBOY

Yeah, don't you forget, old man, if'n we didn' need to leave that town in such a hurry, we'd a' never blown that bank, and we'd a' never had no seven thousand to rest on for a while.

OLD COWBOY

You goddamn guys think it's so goddamn easy!

(The THREE COWBOYS exit downstage left.
The following interludes are played without sets. The BANKER and SHERIFF are as if at a bar; the BANKER'S DAUGHTER as if in her sitting room; the WHORE and MADAM as if in the WHORE'S bedroom. Each interlude is preceded by a tune which is hummed by the heavenly heroes.
Tune: "El Rancho Grande"—hummed spiritedly.)

BANKER

(Turning around, leaning back on bar)
Sheriff, I been banker for this town longer'n you and me care to remember, right?

SHERIFF

(Facing BANKER)
Yessir, that surely is right. Was a heap of years ago we both of us settled down here.

BANKER

And been a lot of water under the dam we don't need to talk about both before and after, right?

SHERIFF

Yessir, you are surely right there, when you say that. Oh me!

BANKER

Well, the way I feel, Sheriff, is, good riddance to bad rubbish. I'm so glad to see those boys gone, that I wouldn't offer no reward nohow for their capture. Why, they liable to get aggravated, either bust out, or wait till they was let out, or, God forbid, beat the charges somehow, and come back here and devil the livin' hell out of all of us, but mostly me and you. I figger seven thousand dollars a cheap price to be rid of them, and besides, the money's probably gone by now, and a reward would just be throwin' good money after bad. Yessir, I was powerful glad to see them leave, even at that price, the way that young skinny one was always hangin' around my daughter.

SHERIFF

Right you are. I surely would feel the same about that, if'n I had a beautiful seventeen-year-old daughter. And what with the mine hittin' the way it is, and the railhead comin' in, so's the drives'll end up here, I guess you got no need to worry about the money. Only thing was, the boys asked me was there a reward and such, and was it worth trackin' them, and so I just had to up and ask you. Wouldn' hardly be fair to my boys nowise if'n I didn't.

BANKER

Well, Sheriff, I surely do understand. And listen, Sheriff, if there's one person in town you don't need to worry about apologizin' to, on account of anythin' you do or done, or might even want to do, it's me. I think you know that, Sheriff, and how much I am beholden to you all we been through in the past.

(Turns back to bar.

Tune: "Beautiful, Beautiful Brown Eyes"—sentimentally.)

BANKER'S BEAUTIFUL DAUGHTER

(Crosses to center stage on platform)

Dear Diary, I think I am honest and truly going to have a baby. And him a bandit. Oh, when he held me in his arms, I could just feel he was a thrilling man. I even asked him once. I said, bold as brass, are you a bandit? No ma'am, he said, not me, but I could feel his arms a-tightening around me when he said it. The only thing is, dear diary, poor Daddy. Won't he have a fit?

(Crosses right, sits on right edge of platform.

Tune: "You Are My Sunshine"—hummed music-hall style.)

MADAM

(Enters downstage left on to platform)

Well, you old whore, I hope you're proud of yourself. Screwed me up somethin' proper you did, hangin' around like that with old fastdraw. Oh he paid all right, but I could've used you, and there you was hangin' round moonin' over him. And me havin' to put up with his damn loud mouth on top of it. I'm damn glad he's gone, I can tell you.

WHORE

Well I'm glad he's gone too. It was gettin' to be awful borin' toward the end, what with him always wantin' me to be standin' by his side all night long while he played poker. Brings him luck, says he. I'll give him luck. But I ought to tell you somethin' else, I reckon, seein' how it concerns you too. I think I give him a dose in addition to the luck.

MADAM

Damn you! I don't know whether to kiss you for fixin' him up, or kick you for screwin' me up. Don't you know there'll be a big drive in soon? You better take it easy for a while, get yourself straightened out. You better go on up to Colorado and see old Manny. I'll give you your fare, but you leave your clothes here, hear? I wonder who it was dosed you up though. Have to ask Doc.

WHORE

I think probably it was that faro dealer was around. I never did trust him.

MADAM

You may be right. Howsomever, it's Colorado for you for a while.

WHORE

Yeah. And all the time I'm up there, I'm goin' to think about the three of them, old quickdraw and the other two, and hope I don't die laughin'. I tell you, I just have to think how puzzled his face get, when I told him what Jane said to me about the banker tellin' her how he was goin' to have the sheriff's boys run the three of them out of town, and I break up laughin'. Those three big gunnies
(COWBOYS *enter from upstage left behind barrier, stand silently to suggest riding*)
runnin' 'cause of a silly little chit like that. But they did have balls enough to rob the banker to do their runnin' on. That much I got to give them credit for.

MADAM

Pshaw. You should've seen the boys I learned from. They would've took the whole damn bank with 'em, and the banker and the banker's daughter too. And wouldn't none of those boys been fool enough to pick up a dose. Would've left that for some other sucker.

(They both laugh and go out.

Tune: "I'm Back in the Saddle Again"—hummed straight.

The desert, noon. It's hot as hell, and there is no shade at all. OLD COWBOY *signals "halt," they all come around barrier on to platform.)*

OLD COWBOY

(Keeps circling)

Unless I miss my guess, there ain't even a bush within ten miles of here. But we better stop anyhow. The horses been goin' more'n an hour steady, and my belly been grumblin' the last two. Gotta eat somethin'.

GUNNY

Damn. Must be two hunnerd and ten degrees out here. You sure we goin' to find a place by night? Even a old rock to sleep my head under?

YOUNG COWBOY

Your head. Your head. Who in hell said your head was so damn important? For an instance, my head's a hell of a lot more important to me than anybody's head, even yours.

OLD COWBOY

Goddamn you two, stop, hear? Ain't nobody's head goin' to be important 'less I find a way out of this. And yes, we are goin' to find a place by tonight. Why you think I roused you so early? And all the while you two were bitchin'. Listen, I been through this desert on horse, in a wagon, in a posse, in front of a posse, and even walkin'. The last would be with that squaw woman I stole from the Arikara. They never come close to catchin' us either. I guess I told you

142

all about that a dozen times or so, though. Anyhow, I know damned well they's a little spot just about maybe four five hours' ride from here, got it a waterhole, grass for the horses, and a tree for each and every one of us for to sleep our heads under.

GUNNY

And probably goddamn Indians too, but you forgot to mention them.

YOUNG COWBOY

A while back, seems to me, you was right happy when he suggested findin' Indians, so's we could buy us some horses, but now you don't even want to see them for to get us a little shade, even.

COMMERCIAL: HORSES ARE ONE OF THE EARLIEST OF
DOMESTICATED ANIMALS

The horse has, for eons, been an integral part of man's civilization and culture. So integral a part, that some say, among them eminent historians, that had the Indian had the horse for three hundred years longer than he did have the horse, his civilization would have developed to the point where he could have withstood the white invasion along the banks of the mighty Mississippi, and contained the United States east of the great natural barrier. Perhaps.

(When lights come up OLD COWBOY *is seated,* GUNNY *stretched out,* YOUNG COWBOY *standing.)*

YOUNG COWBOY
(Walks in circle)

Man, it's surely nothin' much at all around here, is it? Looks like the most whole of nothin' I ever did see.

143

(He reaches in his shirt pocket, pulls out some jerky, takes a chaw, and throws it to OLD COWBOY.)

OLD COWBOY

Thankee, son, mighty kindly of you. Here, have some of this here water, if you will.

(Offers canteen)

Want a chaw of jerky, friend?

(Throws it at GUNNY)

GUNNY

(Throwing it away)

No, I don't want no damn jerky.

(Stands looking around)

Jesus! Almost really do wish I'd see some Indians. Make me feel like somethin' was alive here, besides us three. And I ain't sure we three alive. Fuckin desert, goddamn this fuckin desert.

OLD COWBOY

(To GUNNY)

Don't you worry none about that, boy.

(To YOUNG COWBOY)

Right now, the less people we see the better it goin' to be. By the time we hit a big town, us two goin' to have our beards full grown almost, and ain't even nobody goin' to think we is us. And then we get us a nice hotel room, and set down and count us that money real slow. And then we go out to spend it, but we spend it real easy, and slow as molasses, so nobody goin' to get ideas, and pretty soon all them people goin' to get used to seein' us around, and won't pay us no never mind. And we'll live a long time nice and easy, and then, when we got to, we'll go back to work. Why, I might even look for the sheriff's job, myself. And you boys could be my deputies if you'd a mind to.

BOTH

Deputies!

OLD COWBOY

Why not? I'm gettin' to be that age, I could use a little rest, might be a little bit of fun be a sheriff for a little while, or even a long while. Might marry me a pretty girl, get me a pretty ranch, have me a pretty life.

GUNNY

Oh me. Listen to him go. You be a goddamn old sheriff all you want, but me, I ain't old yet. I got to get me a whole lot of everything before I start pullin' that stuff, hear? But I sure glad to kiss you when you get your badge, and very damn glad to draw on you too, exceptin' that you my friend or that you was.

YOUNG COWBOY

Well, I don't know. I think maybe you talkin' big, you all whipped up right now. But I think they offer either of us a badge, you or me, we both goin' to jump for it, and knock heads jumpin' too. I know damn well I jump. Have it nice and easy that way, never have to do nothin' except maybe once in a while a hardhead like you decide he goin' to drink too much, I got to take you in. Say on a lovely Saturday night you start shoutin' and whoopin' and hollerin', I get my turn to come up and lay you out with one acrost the head, than which, incidentally, nothin' would give me more pleasure, then or now, I might add.

(GUNNY *makes mock bow to* YOUNG COWBOY.)

OLD COWBOY

Look, I might as well straighten you both out right now. I don't want no trouble cookin' here. He

(*Nodding to* YOUNG COWBOY)

knows it as well as me. We both of us seen sign of Arikara this morning at the camp. Any one of you gets feelin' revengeful, it's only goin' to hurt all of us, hisself included. Aside from we're all a little loco with the sun. Them damn injuns could be on our tails right now, we don't keep shakin' them.

(GUNNY *suddenly alerts.*)

COMMERCIAL: THE PRIMITIVE RADAR

Indians were notorious for their ability to track, or follow, other persons unnoticed. They walked very quietly, and could deduce, often, a trail from the most minute evidence. It is a known fact that all the western cavalry regiments, including Custer's, had a complement of Indian trackers to lead them through the wastes. These trackers were generally enlisted from friendly tribes, and did their best to warn our soldiers of the dangers confronting them, from the signs they were able to read along the path of travel.

GUNNY

Well, this is sure a hell of a time to tell a fellow something like that, damn it. What you want me to do?

YOUNG COWBOY

Keep your mouth shut.

GUNNY

Man, I wasn't talking to you. And you don't keep your mouth shut, I'm liable to close it for you. And I mean I do it to you too, hear?

YOUNG COWBOY

Okay, I'm shuttin' up, but only 'cause of Indians, 'cause I know all about you. The only thing you going to do it to or

anythin' is that silly fat old whore you left behind. You
going to do it to that stuff proper. I bet she clapped you up
in the bargain.

GUNNY

(Starts to draw and rushes toward YOUNG COWBOY*)*
You sonofabitch . . .

OLD COWBOY

(Stops GUNNY *with a gesture)*
Man, I think you better make an effort and straighten
yourself out like I told you. You been gettin' worse and
worse as the day pass on. I heard how you been pitching
on the kid all morning. Why'n't you go and do it now, and
get it over with?

GUNNY

Goddamn, maybe I will.
(He exits.)

COMMERCIAL: DOPE, THE DOCTOR'S FRIEND
During the Civil, or War Between the States, or, as
it was sometimes known, the late unpleasantness,
the only means available to surgeons, physicians,
and the like, of alleviating excruciating pain due to
wounds or amputations were the drugs cocaine and
morphine. As a consequence, close to a million men
who had served valiantly found themselves
"hooked" to one extent or another on these drugs
after the close of hostilities. Indeed, there were so
many of these poor addicts that it was impossible
for the government to pass any anti-narcotic legis-
lation till after the turn of the century, when their
numbers had diminished. Most doctors were sym-
pathetic to their plight.

YOUNG COWBOY

It surely do embarrass me when he carry on like that. And then that private thing he got to have. Do he think we going to laugh or something?

OLD COWBOY

Boy, I don't know. All I know is, any man come out of three four months in a hospital during that war, seems like they just got to have that stuff every so often or they just ain't ever goin' to be happy. Reckon I'm glad I wasn't never wounded there in the Shenandoah, or I might be just the same. As it is, a little whiskey now and again keep me satisfied, or a little bit of nooky. But those boys, they got to be a-stickin' that needle in they arm, every now and again, or they is most morose. I can't figure it, but I reckon the doctors can.

YOUNG COWBOY

Only thing bother me, why he got to do it in private. I offer to shoot it for him oncet, he got awful upset. No, he say, goddamn this I got to do myself. Well, I guess I just don't know.

GUNNY

(Re-enters, very relaxed, ready for a nice long talk)
Well, I about ready to roll now. But listen, what you done with that there jerky? Sure am gettin' a little bit of hungry here. Been ridin' all this long time and ain't had nothin' to eat. And seems like I been growin' a powerful hunger.

YOUNG COWBOY

Here's the jerky, friend. Eat well. And here's the canteen.

GUNNY

Thankee, friend. You boys are sure a good bunch of boys to be ridin' with. Minds me of the time we rode down into Alabam' with Uncle Billy. I was ridin' with as fine a bunch you ever hope to see, ride here, ride there, ride every-where, and find us the finest ladies, and the finest food, and the finest of everything your little heart ever dreamed of. Sure was a fine time ridin' like that, till I got wounded. And even that wasn't so bad, long as they had those damn nee-dles around. Only difference twixt us and them, was then we sure had a powerful lot of people ridin' with us.

OLD COWBOY

Well I wouldn't worry about that none, was I you. You're with friends, and that's a heap better than bein' in the mid-dle of a whole bunch of boys ridin' one way and another and wavin' swords and things. Why'n't you two shake just to show there's no hard feelings?

GUNNY

Fine by me. I like the young'un a heap. Here.
(They shake.)

YOUNG COWBOY

Sure, boy. You know you are the pleasantest fellow in the world with that stuff in you.
(Takes canteen and toasts)
Here's to it. And to you. And to us.

OLD COWBOY

Okay, boys, now that's settled let's finish up here and get the hell out.
(Rises and goes upstage right)
I want to be safe in that old waterhole before the sun gets close to settin'. Man, when I think of the time that old squaw and me had there, I'll tell you. And after walkin' all day long too, in the burnin' sun. Well I ain't gettin' any younger.

YOUNG COWBOY

That's a fact. Fact is, ain't none of us gettin' any younger.

That there banker's daughter, why she had me feelin' like a old grandpa sometimes, and me only twenty-two. Whoeee! That little girl sure didn't want to hear no noes out of me.

GUNNY

That's the way it is with those young'uns sometimes. But one day, say somewhere around me and my old gray-haired thirty-five, you goin' to find out how restful and easy it is to give that young stuff up and just pick yourself out a nice silly fat whore, like the one I got me. She don't expect no wonders, and she just happy you is there.

YOUNG COWBOY

Well, I'm beginnin' to think maybe you might be right. But I think I'll wait a bit to find out. The young'uns got their points, too, don't forget.

OLD COWBOY

You boys can sit around like that all afternoon if you've a mind to, but me I'm goin' to skedaddle.
(Goes behind barrier, upstage right)

GUNNY

Hold on there, we're with you, right?

YOUNG COWBOY

Right.

OLD COWBOY

Okay. Here's what I say. We string ourselves out maybe six lengths apart, so they can't get us all at once, if'n they come, but we're still close enough to join up if'n we have to. And most of all, we make those horses move. Agreed?
(Moves to upstage left behind barrier)

GUNNY

That sure does sound right to me. Damn! I'm sure glad you leadin' the fuckin way. By this time I don't even know

150

which way to head, sun or no sun. I don't even remember which goddamn sonofabitch way is east anymore, or south or west or north, for that matter.

(Moves to upstage center behind barrier)

YOUNG COWBOY
(Packing up.)

I sure hope, old pals, we ain't headin' west.

OLD COWBOY

Talk like that ain't goin' to get us no place. Only thing will is ridin' leather, makin' dust. Let's hit it. I know just which way that little old waterhole lays.

YOUNG COWBOY
(Moves while speaking to upstage right behind barrier)

Yeah, but I sure do hope we ain't headin' west. I'm much too young for that. I got to find out 'bout them fat silly old whores. I sure hope we ain't headin' west yet, or leastwise me.

(LIGHTS DIM DOWN. THREE COWBOYS *are visible standing behind barrier as if riding, through interlude.*
Tune: "Red River Valley"—powerfully.
LIGHTS UP bright on heaven.)

WYATT EARP
(Rises)

Boys, this here is Wyatt Earp speakin' from up here in heaven. I sure hope all you fellows are doin' your best to do your part. That's what I wanted to talk to you about today. *Doin' your part.* I know there are some around today who'll try and tell you boys I was a psychopath, because, they'll say, I liked to lop my buntline special, all that big long barrel, across some baddie's face but boys, I was just doin' my part as I saw fit. The West had to be made fit to live in, and by providence I was the man picked to do my part. There's no denyin' that all that shootin' and killin' and hootin' and hollerin' wasn't fun too, but most of all it was plain and simple, doin' my part. Boys, what I got to say to you is, like it says in the good book: go thou and do likewise.

(Sits)

WILD BILL HICKOK

(Congratulates WYATT, *then stands)*

All right, boys, I decided it was time I give you the one and only truth about myself, old Wild Bill Hickok. First of all it's true Bill wasn't my proper first handle, but that's what they called me. So now up here in heaven I call me that too. And it's surely true, boys, that all that stuff about the notches in my gun was just somethin' I made up to impress a smart alecky New York reporter. But I done my share of fightin' in my day, and I'm here to tell you. I know there's a lot around today who wasn't never there who'll deny that last, call me a fraud, and what hurts more, they even sayin' there must of been somethin' queer about me. Boys, I put it to you, if'n I liked my hair shoulder long, and my linen a little fancy and spotless clean, and never did go out with none of those whores like the rest of the boys, boys, whose business is that 'ceptin' mine? It's my affair and none of their own. All you boys got to remember is that I were the best trick shot in the West. Why those same people, they always pointin' to my dainty well-formed hands but boys, from up here in heaven, I can just say I was blessed with them. They sure helped me in my trade, bein' the best trick shot in the West.

(Sits. WYATT *congratulates him.)*

BILLY THE KID

(Rises, stares tensely around heaven, and stage, and audience all through speech)

Well, boys, up here in heaven, where they put me, even

though it's some special section I can't seem to get out of, out there with the others, not even when I can see plain as day that yellow sneakin' bastard Pat Garrett a-sneakin' around just like he did when he come sneakin' in my bedroom while I was just tryin' to catch a little wink, and so goddamn dark I couldn't even see to draw on him, goddamn they ain't goin' to do this to Billy the Kid, not even up here in heaven, just 'cause I come from hell's kitchen they act like I was the first J.D. or somethin'. Oh yes I know what they sayin' about me, calling me a goddamn J.D. just like I was some fuckin P.R., or shade or somethin', man I'll burn those mothers, all of them, they come pokin' their holier-than-thou noses in here, up in heaven. Mothers.

(Sits)

DOC HOLLIDAY
(Rises. He coughs continually through the speech.)
Well boys, this is the old con man, the original hipster, the first of the hackin' hipsters talkin' to you from up here in heaven. Yes boys, it's true, we're all up here. All them you heard and a lot more besides. Last two we, or rather they let in, they said it were the last of the heroes. That'd be, I know you're interested, Butch Cassidy and the Sundance Kid. Now wasn't that twosome a bitch? Oh man. Well, anyhow, here what old Doc got to tell you. (1) You got to live like you goin' to die next month anyhow. (2) You got to be a good gambler, that means learn the rules, and have you some luck. (3) You got to take time out to learn you a trade, for the bad times, the slow times, and when you got to cool it.
(Lights on COWBOYS full out. They take next position in BLACKOUT.)
You just do these three things, boys, you ain't goin' to have no trouble a-tall findin' yourself some upright crazy sonofa-

bitch like Wyatt to pick up on, and then, boys, you goin' to have a ball. You goin' to be able to kick up such hell out of a sweet lovin' bitch like big nose Bertha on Monday night that she have you thrown in jail. And you goin' to be able to fill her with so many memories, that Tuesday night she goin' to burn down the jail, and have your horse waitin' for you outside the window, so's the two of you can ride off into the desert. One more thing, boys, pure fact, John Ringo *is* dead. I seen Wyatt plug him, and threw in two myself for luck. Okay boys, that's about it. You hearken unto what I said and cleave your hearts unto it until next time, boys, this is Doc Holliday sayin' so long for all of us
    (Waves)
up here in heaven.
    (LIGHTS DIM on heaven. COWBOYS *are seated upstage left.)*

    YOUNG COWBOY

Damn! I'm surely sick and tired of all you screwing around whilst I make meals, and then just wolfin' them down, and nary a word about was they good, was they bad, was they indifferent, or what?

    OLD COWBOY

Looky here, we ain't been screwin' around. We been gettin' the damn wood for the fire, and some soft branches for to sleep on, and afeedin' and awaterin' the horses, and hobblin' them, and all. And in betwixt, we been lookin' for sign of Arikara. So you stop that whoopin'. You got no call at all to come on in that there manner.

    GUNNY

Yeah, goddamn it.
    (He belches.)

    YOUNG COWBOY

Well, that's just how I feel. I know I ain't got much to cook with here, but you boys could at least hearken back to the time I had the wherewithal. It's damned hard to have to cook all the time like this, and get no praise nor thanks nor even bitches. I think you boys don't even taste it, and me breakin' my hump just to get it to taste like food, even.

GUNNY

All right, all right. It tasted like food see. That's all it's supposed to taste like, and that's all it did taste like. It tasted like food. What the hell you expect? Ain't neither of us married to you yet, goddamn it. I'm so goddamned sick of your bitchin', and his leaderin' and my goddamn ridin'.

OLD COWBOY

You sick of it, yeah, but you was damn glad I was around when we started seein' those smoke signals, wasn't you.

(*A coyote howls. They all fall silent, sit for a minute.* OLD COWBOY *assigns positions for defense.*)

OLD COWBOY

(*Whispering*)

This may be it, boys. Good luck, and a good fight, and if that's all, then goodbye, boys. You been a fine bunch to ride with. But I'll bet my bottom dollar on it, that sounded powerful like Arikara.

COMMERCIAL: THE INDIANS OF THE AMERICAS A VERI-
TABLE TOWER OF BABEL

The Indians of the Americas are unique in their considerable diversity of tongues. Over seventy different language families have been discovered, amongst the Indians of North America alone. A family of languages is, in linguistic terms, a group of fairly similar languages between which various ties of vocabulary and syntax are apparent. The

155

Indo-European family, for instance, comprises most of the inhabitants of Europe, and a good third of those of Asia. Imagine then the great diversity of languages to be found in early America, before the Indians were killed off. The Arikara belonged to one of these seventy language families.

GUNNY

Listen, you supposed that might've been a real coyote, anyhow? It's about time for them to be comin' out, around about now.

OLD COWBOY

Well, it could've been. And there weren't no answer. And, come to think of it, that damn yowl wasn't really real enough for Arikara. They sound realer than coyote most of the time.

YOUNG COWBOY

I ain't heard too many Indians signalin' but I know that's true.
(Starts to rise, is motioned at, crouches)
Leastwise it's what I heard from a lot of fellows.

OLD COWBOY

Well, let's relax a little, boys; most they can do is kill us. Long as it ain't a damn posse anyhow. Indians ain't goin' to know we gotta damn seven thousand in our saddlebags, and Arikara sure ain't smart enough to look. They'll just scalp us and take the guns and throw us all on the fire, or they'll leave us layin'. Dependin' on the fight we put up. I know it may be silly but I'd damn sight rather the money stays with us dead, than somebody else gets it and spends it.

YOUNG COWBOY

Yeah. After what that fuckin banker tried to pull on us just because his damn beautiful daughter liked her tail, I feel the same.

GUNNY

Well, I hate to mention it to you, but if I had my druthers, I'd a heap better like spendin' it myself than knowin' nobody else had it. Though I would like knowin' that better than knowin' somebody else did have it. That is, if we are goin' to know anythin' after we're dead. And I ain't so sure of that.

OLD COWBOY

Now you know as well as I do ain't no sense worryin' about that sort of thing. That's the preacher's lookout, and he says we're goin' to know. That's good enough for me.

YOUNG COWBOY

And that's the way I feel too. I got nothin' to be ashamed of, when they read that final list, then the last trump blow, like the preacher say.

(Silence—thought)

OLD COWBOY

I been meaning to say to you, boy, you a good cook. If the good Lord ever see fit to let me have that little ranch I keep dreamin' about, I goin' to let you cook for me any old time you want. You didn't have much to work with, but you made us a good old supper. Like the feller said, it were the best shit I ever ate.

YOUNG COWBOY

Well, that's mighty fine to hear. I'm surely glad you enjoyed it. And I want to tell you, I sort of enjoyed fixin' it up. It was a nice change after all day in the saddle.

GUNNY

Pardner, I got to say it too. For me it was a nice change to

have food in my goddamn gut. I get so damn hungry sometimes after I have me that medicine, I don't know what to
do. I appreciate what you doin' for us. I want to tell you
that.

YOUNG COWBOY

You boys going to make me shy. Thanks, thanks a whole lot
of millions.

OLD COWBOY

Well, I'm goin' to make a last check on the horses. Sure
hope I don't find no sound around this time.
(Exits upstage left. YOUNG COWBOY *covers his position.)*

GUNNY

And me, I'm goin' to turn in. I'm tired. Been all day in
the saddle and I'm wore out.
(Throws rifle to YOUNG COWBOY*)*
Boy, you call me when breakfast ready, you hear?
(Starts undressing)

YOUNG COWBOY
(Alert and apprehensive)
I goin' to call you when and how I get goddamn ready,
damn you! Who you think you are to get a goddamn special call? All you do is ride, sleep, eat, and . . .
(Cooling down)
I got to add, draw faster nor any man got a right to. Where'd
you learn that little trick? I been meanin' to ask you. I know
for a fact your old man so slow he won't even draw on a
man in handcuffs.

GUNNY

Boy, you know you ain't about to rile me when I'm ready
to sleep. Though it was true my old man was slow. I mind
me of the time he caught me with sister. I was but twelve,

but I faced him down even then. I had my Colt a-pointin' at his heart afore he even got his gun out. And that's how I left home, youngster. Oh, those goddamned good old never-come-again fuckin old days, I sure wish I was twenty again.

(Lies down)

YOUNG COWBOY

Way I left, I left middle of the night. Paw had got drunk that day and whupped me. I swore it were the last time. Old man was so loaded his snorin' covered every sound I made. But somehow, Maw heard me out to the barn. She come out in her old wrapper, and man, it were cold. She give me some food, and a kiss goodbye.

(OLD COWBOY re-enters, stands upstage left off platform.)

I told her I was takin' the mule but when she run back to the house I took the best mare. You never seen that mare. She died four year ago, but she was surely a sweet old horse. And I had my daddy's Colt in my shirt too, whilst I was kissin' Mama goodbye. And by damn I learned to use them both, Colt and mare, I tell you.

OLD COWBOY

You are speakin' truth, boy, you can do it when you need to.

(Undresses)

I just wish you felt a need to, more. But pay no mind to that. That's just an old man's talk. You goin' to come out all right. You goin' to have everything your heart desires some day, boy. And the sun goin' to shine in your back door. The other two of us, I ain't so sure. But you goin' to make it.

(Lies down)

GUNNY

Okay, boys, hush it up. I need my beauty sleep if I'm going

to be ridin' all around this countryside all day tomorrow on nothin' but bacon and beans and coffee.

OLD COWBOY

Me too. Good night, you all.

GUNNY

Goddamn, good night.

YOUNG COWBOY

Well, I'll hit it too. Though I guess us young'uns is too lively for you old goats. 'Cause I ain't really tired yet. But I do have me a powerful lot of thinkin' to do about that damn old banker's beautiful daughter, anyhow, and I'd sure rather do that thinkin' alone, without you guys to share it.

(There is no answer. They are both asleep. He sits upstage center on platform.)

They may get us or maybe not. And tomorrow I got to ride like hell. And I'm tired, damn you. But first I'm goin' to sing me a little song.

(While he sings LIGHTS DIM on stage, LIGHTS GO UP bright on heaven, both very gradually.)

> I ride an Old Paint
> I ride an Old Paint,
> I lead an Old Dan,
> I'm goin' to Montana
> To throw the houlihan.
>
> They feed in the tuli,
> They water in the draw,
> Their tails are all matted,
> Their backs are all raw.

(HEAVENLY HEROES *hum softly behind Chorus only:)*

Ride round, little dogies,
Ride round them real slow,
You know that Wyoming will be your new home.
Ride round, little dogies,
Ride round them real slow,
Both Fiery and Snuffy are rarin' to go.

Now old Tom Jones
Had two daughters and a song;
One went to Denver,
The other went wrong.

His wife was killed
In a poolroom fight,
Now Tom sits asinging
From morning to night.

(Chorus:)

Now when I die
Take my saddle from the wall
Turn loose my pony
From out of his stall,

Put my bones across his back,
Turn our faces to the west,
And we'll ride the prairies
That we love the best.

(He sleeps.)

COMMERCIAL: INDIAN MORALS, A STRICT ETHICAL CODE
Indians had a strict moral code. They respected
courage and manliness, despised cowardice. For a

plains, or desert, Indian, the supreme test was brav-
ery under torture. In addition, Indians never at-
tacked after dark. It was against their moral code.

(GUNNY *rises and stumbles about on the dark stage.*)

GUNNY

Goddamn! It can't be mornin'. But I got to take such a
fierce pee. And it hurts something awful. It hurts so bad I
could bend a pipe.

(BLACKOUT)

THE END

LA MAMA EXPERIMENTAL THEATRE CLUB

ELLEN STEWART, founder of La Mama.

La Mama E.T.C. is an experimental theatre club, dedicated to the playwright and all aspects of the theatre. That tells everything.

I wanted to create a premise out of which creative theatre experimentation could best be served, and I think there is a subliminal rapport that somehow has come into being here, with the playwright or the production and the audience. It eliminates the separation of artist and audience that one is so aware of in "contemporary" theatre. The playwrights I'm interested in write on a subconscious level, and this in effect has evolved into a "new theatre"—a new entity. The new theatre is much more subliminal, more subconscious. We have LSD, peyote, mescaline, all these things for brain searching. I don't mean you take these things and write; it's more than that. But because of them we have become much more aware and acute on a subconscious level.

We have an audience intensely interested in theatre. They're not coming for thrills and shocks, they're coming because they're interested in theatre. Our atmosphere has spoiled Broadway and Off-Broadway for them. There, all the things they feel come a day or two later, when they discuss it with someone. Here they feel the theatrical event right away, it gets inside them. It opens them, they can feel it and take it in. People in their fifties and sixties aren't attuned to this, but the gap is fast closing. The majority of our audience are settled people who want to find out about and experience this new thing.

Criticism as to the noncomprehensibility of the works offered comes invariably from the audience person who has yet to recognize the subconscious stimuli. (This is the only way I know to express these things. Nobody is going to believe I said this—but this is the way I feel, and I feel very strongly about this.)

He suddenly finds that he is not in tune. And he is goaded by these plays into doing something about it. Whatever techniques are used, the audience person in spite of himself tries to understand, and this he achieves to some degree. He may or may not keep and use this understanding, but often he does, which is demonstrated by his constant return to the source. I personally find this a great joy, because it is a sign that today's civilization is not going to stagnate. I like plays that can be done on an abstract level. This is what theatre is going to be, and the world is going to have to get ready for it. Because we're old and we're jaded, and we have to get underneath—we really have to stimulate the subconscious. The artist has always been the prophet of mankind, and it is evident in the writings of the new playwrights that society for its survival must become oriented to exercising its imagination to the utmost. That is exactly what the new playwrights are doing. The plays that we're doing are the plays I want to do. I don't interfere in how they get to be that way. I'm here to serve the playwright—and I feel this is the best way he can be served, whether he knows it or not.

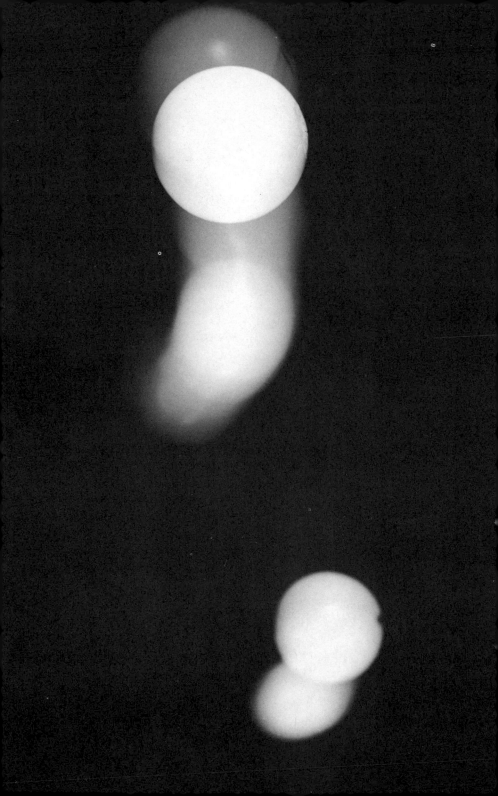

Balls

by Paul Foster

BALLS had its première at La Mama Experimental Theatre Club on November 3, 1964. It was directed by Sydney Schubert Walter with the following cast:

"COMMODORE" WILKINSON	Paul Boesing
BEAU BEAU	James Barbosa
BUS DRIVER	Sydney Walter
MISS MC CUTCHEON	Shirley Stoler
NASTY BRAT	Anthony Bastiano
YOUNG LOVERS	Paul Boesing
	Shelly Feldman
THE WOMAN WHO HAD NO SHADOW	Claire Leyba
MILITARY COMMANDER	James Barbosa
STEREO ENGINEER	Norman Long
ORIGINAL MUSIC	Gary William Friedman
STAGE MANAGER	Lola Richardson

PAUL FOSTER *was born in Pennsgrove, New Jersey, and holds a B.A. from Rutgers University. He has had three one-act plays and one three-act play produced Off-Off Broadway.* Hurrah for the Bridge *played at the Caffe Cino and Cafe La Mama in 1963. It was translated and performed in Spanish and German; in English and Spanish it was published in Bogota, Colombia, in 1964, with an introduction by Sydney Schubert Walter.* The Recluse *was produced by Ellen Stewart at the Village South Theatre in 1964 and subsequently at La Mama. It was performed on La Mama Repertory's tour of Paris, Sweden, and Denmark in 1965–1966 and included in the Off-Broadway production of* Six from La Mama *at the Martinique Theatre.* Balls *premièred at La Mama and later moved to the Caffe Cino and the Cherry Lane Theatre, where it was part of the Albee-Barr-Wilder New Playwrights' Series.* The Madonna in the Orchard, *Foster's first three-act play, was performed at Cafe La Mama in November 1965, at Sundance Theater and at the Eugene O'Neill Theater in July 1966.*

Balls

by Paul Foster

SET

A black-curtained stage. Two white ping pong balls hang suspended on invisible wires about mid-height or lower and well within the depth of the stage. One on the left. One on the right. Two stationary, small, white spotlights on either end are focused on the transits of the two balls so that the balls swing in and out of the lights' paths. The visual entirety is a black immensity with the balls emerging from the wings, swinging slowly toward each other, disappearing-reappearing into the light sources. When finally they touch, they begin to separate again and recede slowly to their respective sides until they disappear finally into the blackness of the wings.

All voices and sounds are taped and come from above us offstage. The players speak in coarse whispers, so integrated with the sea sound that their whispers seem to wash toward us from a great distance.

TIME

A foggy night.

PLACE

A cemetery by the sea. An ancient place. The sea has washed away the land and claimed all the graves except two.

THE PLAYERS:

"COMMODORE" WILKINSON, *the voice of an old man, phlegmatic, deep, and coarsely textured. There is strength in it. He whispers slowly and projects the feeling that his voice requires time to travel a great distance to reach us.*

169

BEAU BEAU, *the voice of a mature younger man. It is quicker and more spirited. He whispers too but it always seems more present to us.*

MISS MCCUTCHEON, *the voice of a high-strung, nervous woman.*

BUS DRIVER, *the pedestrian-accented, deep voice of a man.*

YOUNG LOVERS, *the voices of male and female animals in heat.*

THE MILITARY COMMANDER, *the strong voice of authority.*

THE WOMAN WHO HAD NO SHADOW, *a beer-encrusted voice, brittle, hard, and coarse.*

NASTY BRAT, *the intolerably innocent-evil voice of a six-year-old boy.*

A GANGLIA OF HIGH-PITCHED CHILDREN.

THE SOUNDS

The sea. A military march of drums, slow paced, sharp. A player piano, rapid firing of joyous notes. A bus. Passage of water. A bosun's whistle. Rain and thunder. A bell buoy.

(Black. The sea insinuates. A bell buoy. 30 seconds. From an infinite distance, martial drums approach. The voice is deep, phlegmatic, strong in old age. He whispers.)

WILKINSON

This wreck of a ship underfoot. Flying jib to spanker, full up. Sounding line a cunt's hair to first mark. Put up another leg-of-mutton and sprits. Look like? Look like? OH, GET ON WITH YOUR WORK, MAN! Gunnels gone, we at first mark and the stink of cannon sulphur fair to snuff us all. What's she look like?! Look like? GET ON, MAN!

(Drums pass into the distance. The sea rolls unperturbed throughout and is left alone now. 15 seconds. A heavy sigh.)

Ah, these memories, these ghosts.

(Pause)

Yes . . . get on with it!

(Two small white spotlights pop on simultaneously at the command. The sea recedes quietly in the back and rolls throughout.)

Get on!

(From the left the first ball swings out, appearing-disappearing into the light. Pause. He follows its transit.)

Smartly now. *Hup* two. *Hup* two. *Hup* two. *Hup* . . .

(Pause)

You too.

(Long pause)

Fall into step. *Hup* two. *Hup* two. *Hup* . . .

(Pause)

Get on!

(The second ball swings out, appearing-disappearing into the light. The two swing slowly, silently, imperceptibly toward each other. Pause. Only the roll of the sea.

A burst of bright, dance-hall, player-piano music. 15 seconds. It stops abruptly. He sings immediately, jocosely dissonant, rapid fire, cocky as a red feather.)

BEAU BEAU

> I am a pretty wench,
> And I come a great way hence,
> And sweethearts I can get none:
> > But every dirty sow
> > Can get sweethearts enou;
> And I pretty wench can get none.

(Pause. Flatly)

Yes, she was a ragged bitch.

WILKINSON

Late as usual.

BEAU BEAU

(Sarcastically)

So sorry.

WILKINSON
As usual.
(Pause)
Well, get in line and fall into step. *Hup* two. *Hup* two.
Hup two. *Hup* two. *Hup* two.

BEAU BEAU
(Over his count)
It's the fog. Slows them down. Always does.

WILKINSON
Late is late no matter how it's turned.

BEAU BEAU
The night don't help none either. Blackens up the fog.
Makes it heavier than day fog.

WILKINSON
(With finality)
Late is late!

BEAU BEAU
Then fug the fog!
(Muttering)
"Late is late," huh!
(Pause)

WILKINSON
Hup two. *Hup* two. *Hup* two.
(BEAU BEAU *sighs heavily. His boredom is apparent. He sings
a droning song.)*

BEAU BEAU
> Two poor devils we are, great burdens we bear,
>> On which we are bitterly pressed;
> The truth is to say, we are full all the day,
>> And empty when we go to rest.

172

WILKINSON

Easy . . . *easy*! Babble on and you'll get them tangled. Then it's trouble to square them away again. *Hup* two. *Hup* two. *Hup* two.

TOGETHER

Steady . . . steady . . .
(Pause)

WILKINSON

Here we lie side by side. An ancient bone pile by the sea. We eat the land. The land eats us. Then the sea eats everything. A fieldful have slipped away with the shore. Blackened ships manned by blackened bones set into a calm black earth. Nothing left now. No jib. No spanker. No leg-of-mutton sail even. To chew? To *gnaw* more like it. TO GNAW!
(Pause)
Cleave through to the raw, naked shore. GNAW THROUGH! A length of blackened box a century. Slow progress. But we get to the waves in time. The others did. A fieldful did. And soon we'll set to drift, you and me. Prisoners borne on a prison ship from a prison earth to a prison sea. From locked keep to locked keep. Then?
(Pause)
Oh, then . . . more of the same. A lovely diet to gnaw. Dead to the second power. We go, a piece at a time. They're all gone now. All except us.

BEAU BEAU
(Quickly)
Us and a nasty pair of balls. I AM so tired of them.
(A loud burst of player piano. 10 seconds. A mighty, resounding slam. It is silenced.)

WILKINSON
(Coolly)
That-ends-that. Will you get her out of your mind?

BEAU BEAU
(With controlled anger)
One hundred and three thousand, two hundred and TWO
times you've blown yours out. One hundred and three thou-
sand, two hundred and TWO times I've blown mine out.
Once a night. AND I'M MUCKING TIRED OF IT!

WILKINSON
(Coolly, matter of fact)
And you were late on every game.

BEAU BEAU
Well, it was one-sweet-hell-of-a-lot-*better*-when-the-others-
played! No rules. One great free-for-all. Hundreds of 'em
all going which way. Carter came out first. Always Carter!
Lean second. BUMP HIM! SMASH HIM A GOOD ONE!
HERE!
(Intermittent grunting with the effort)
BUMP HIM! Easy . . . A GOAL! SIMPSON! SIMPSON!
GET RID OF IT, YOU ASS! RUN IT IN! RUN IT!
(Delighted, excited squeals)
Hundreds of them all going which way. Back and forth,
up and down, in and out, round and round. You never did
know who scored what. WHAT A GLORIOUS MESS!

WILKINSON
(Oblivious to him)
Not a piece of chiseled stone left to say who was who.

BEAU BEAU
Ahhh, many a good player in the lot, say that much for
them.

174

WILKINSON

The sea ate the shore, and they slipped out under the stars in the night. Past the big and little dogs. Over the sickle, chasing the lynx in the spring.

BEAU BEAU

(A growing nervous, forced excitement)

There was Carter, a good boy Carter. Remember him? Pimply-faced, snot-picking kid in knickers.

WILKINSON

(Pressing on calmly, imperturbable)

Warm and black as pitch it was, except for the constellations. A whole section slid out in '85, running after the strong jock up there who chased the lion. Thunder to break your ears in the storm.

BEAU BEAU

(Quicker, louder, his insistence growing)

. . . a kid in knickers who begged to hear about my woman . . . she had no shadow.

WILKINSON

(Unhurried)

The lion . . . the hairy beast fell in the crater. Clawed away, pounded out a great chunk of it . . .

BEAU BEAU

A white, skinny, celery stalk . . .

WILKINSON

(On like a ponderous wave)

. . . a slushy, soggy, rain-sodden soup of earth slid off. Ah, maybe it is the stars that say who will go and who will stay.

BEAU BEAU

(Fully angry at last. Loudly)

175

. . . a white, skinny, celery stalk for a Johnnyo he pumped on when I told the story!

WILKINSON
(A final softly spoken conclusion)
Here we lie.

BEAU BEAU
SHE HAD NO SHADOW!
(The player piano bursts in. 10 seconds. BEAU BEAU *mutters and clicks it off himself.)*
Oh, turn it off. What's the use.

WILKINSON
Steady . . . steady . . .

BEAU BEAU
(A rapid burst of defiant song)
> I know a girl from Bango City,
> She strikes matches on her titty!

WILKINSON
(With slow calm as though he has reached the end of a hymn)
Steady she goes.

BEAU BEAU
DAMN YOU!!
(Long pause. The sea rolls. From the distance a bus approaches, comes to a halt with a gnashing of gears and at once a boisterous ganglia of children shout and gang out.)

BUS DRIVER
Go on. Out, out. Piss on your shoes, then tread all over my bus. Go on, you little bastards.
(A whistle, thin, weakly blown. A woman's voice, maternal, trying to be authoritative, not succeeding. Shouts of jubilant children continue every which way.)

MISS MC CUTCHEON

Two minutes, children. Girls over here. Boys over there.
(Whistle, weakly again)
Two minutes . . . TWO . . . oh, oh . . . darn!
*(Shouts, treading feet, a muffled, quick thudding on the sod.
Then, all quiet. Pause. A small trickle. Pause. An embar-
rassed young giggle. Pause. Many, many trickles begin until
it is oceanic.)*
Turn and face the other way, children.

NASTY BRAT

Miss McCutcheon . . .

MISS MC CUTCHEON

Oh! MIND-THAT-FLASHLIGHT! YOU NASTY
BRAT!
*(Squealing laughter and the thunderous thudding of little
feet. Whistle again, frantic but weak)*
Back to the bus. Bus up, children. BUS UP!
(Whistle. Bus begins to start.)

BUS DRIVER

Come on, little bastards. Get in.
(They thunder into the bus)

MISS MC CUTCHEON

Give that flashlight here.
*(A good resounding crack. Bawling. Door slams. Bus takes
off gnashing its gears. Bus disappears. Pause.)*

BEAU BEAU

Hmmmmmmmm.
(Pause)
It's touching how thoughtful they are. Every spring picnic
they never forget to stop and water the grass.
(Pause)

177

"Little" Miss McCutcheon has a bladder like a cow. She cocks up her leg and lets me have it dead center.

(BEAU BEAU *roars.* WILKINSON *chuckles. It goes into a rasping fit of coughing.*)

WILKINSON

Easy . . . easy, fool! EASY! They're off again. Steady . . . steady . . .

TOGETHER

. . . steady . . . steady.
(Pause)

WILKINSON

You start them off every time.

BEAU BEAU

CHRRRRIST, I AM SO TIRED OF THEM! Go off course. Fall down. Tangle. Explode. Collide. Spill out their guts. SOMETHING! Dong dong, *dong dong,* DONG DONG! DO SOMETHING, YOU MOTHERS!

WILKINSON

Steady . . . steady, old dog.
(Pause)
They are. Swinging back and forth, back and forth. Simple . . . smooth . . . hollow . . . perfect shape. Whole. Complete complete. One to mark time. The other to let it know it's doing a good job. Moving? No. They're not balls. They're an exegesis.

BEAU BEAU

Those exe . . . exe . . . THOSE BALLS make me crosseyed. What are they here for? Who invited them?

WILKINSON
(Sweetly)

178

Then they're not here. Don't think about them and they'll go away. Close your eyes. We'll turn out the lights.

(Pause)

OUT!

(The lights snap out at the command. Black.)

Are your eyes closed? Are they?

BEAU BEAU

Closed they're closed!

WILKINSON

(To the rhythm of the swinging)

Mark time. *Hup* two. *Hup* two. *Hup* two. Have you stopped thinking about them?

BEAU BEAU

(Annoyed)

I-am-trying-not-to, "Commodore" sir.

WILKINSON

Good. Then open your eyes.

(Pause)

Well?

BEAU BEAU

(Hesitant. Whispering)

I . . . I think . . . Wilkinson! Willy, they . . . they. It worked. It worked!

WILKINSON

(Dripping sweetness)

Well now, that is something, isn't it? Beau Beau, let us just put it to the acid test and see, shall we? On. ON!

(Lights on at once. Balls swing as before.)

BEAU BEAU

(Under his breath)

Little bastards.

(WILKINSON *a hoary hoarse laugh*)

OUT! OUT! Turn them out. Leave me alone. You did it. TRESPASSING! Let me alone in my box!

(WILKINSON'S *tone changes completely*)

WILKINSON

Your box. Your gaudy geegaw box.

BEAU BEAU

Go on. Eat your heart out. Teak and rosewood, solid brass fittings and red plush cushions all around in here. The sachet of roses still sweetens it up.

WILKINSON

It smells like a bawdy house. A whore's nightmare she bought by flopping up her scabby legs at fifty cents a throw. She bought it for her pet pimp. That's your gaudy geegaw box.

BEAU BEAU

And what have you got there, "Commodore," eh? Huh, the hero. I don't believe it. I never did. Pine slabs slapped together with horseshoe nails. Military grave? We never saw any trooping the colors over there. Only Miss McCutcheon. trooping her bladder up and down.

WILKINSON

That's enough!

BEAU BEAU

The hero!

(BEAU BEAU *laughs and sings smart and sassy*)

  Don't want a bullet up me arse 'ole,
  Don't want me buttocks shot away . . .

WILKINSON

THAT'S ENOUGH!

BEAU BEAU

> Call out the army and the navy,
> Call out the rank and file,
> Call out me old mother, me sister and me brother,
> But for God's sake, don't call MEEEE.

(BEAU BEAU *roars.* WILKINSON *grunting as though trying to rise up. Thunder. The sea grows louder, more agitated.*)

WILKINSON

CARTER! CARTER'S THE ONE! TOLD EVERY-THING ABOUT YOU!

BEAU BEAU

Carter? Carter? A joke. Never was a Carter. They crapped in a sack and buried it. That's Carter for you.

WILKINSON

(With finality)

And Carter got it from Simpson!

BEAU BEAU

(With paced measure)

Simpson. Simpson? Puh! I'll tell you a story about Simpson. A preacher painted his barn red enamel. The farmer's crosseyed cow sniffed the paint and had a red enameled miscarriage. The farmer flogged the cow for having improper relations with a minister of God. He buried her sin under a false name. A crosseyed, red enameled miscarriage! That's Simpson for you!

WILKINSON

(Faster and faster, totaling up the evidence)

And Simpson got it from Hodges and Hodges got it from Bowen and Bowen got it from Lowry and Lowry got it from Hummel and Hummel got it from Bates and Bates got it from Kinsey and Kinsey got it from Ardsfarth and . . .

BEAU BEAU
Who?

WILKINSON
ARDSFARTH!

BEAU BEAU
(Meekly)
Oh.

WILKINSON

And ARDSFARTH got it from Sweeney and Sweeney got it from Killmer and Killmer got it from Dill and . . .

BEAU BEAU
(Disparagingly)
Oh, Dill. DILL! Who ever listened to DILL?
(Chuckles superiorly)
Him give a clear account of anything. How could he? He only had one leg.
(From the distance approach a woman's high-pitched giggle and a man's husky laugh. The sea sounds are suspended entirely.)
Ahhh, here's the part I like.

WILKINSON
(Disgusted)
Oh, God help us.
(This scene operates independently, like a negative photograph in a line of positives. Each sound is clear and sharp. YOUNG LOVERS. The laughter is conversational. Each makes a statement. The other replies with his laugh. It progresses from high-spirited excitement as they run toward us to an uncertain tapering when they stop. Then each, a deep-breathing exhaustion. A protest; sensuous teasing. Ecstasy of anticipation; cautious determination. Pleasure-pain of

anticipation; an iron determination. Fear. An awful fear. A fall. Tearing. Slapping. Moaning laugh; uncontrolled guttural rasp.)

SHE

Oh . . . God. MOTHER!

HE

Ssssh.
(At once the sea loudly. Pleasure, pain, determination, protest, fear, weave. Thunder, rain, sea loudly. 10 seconds.

The balls touch and begin to recede at once back to their respective corners again at the same tempo. Each hymnlike, a drowsy humming of finality.

All sounds recede to half volume. Long pause.)

HE

(Flat, husky-voiced, slowly with effort)
Oh, here's a grave marker. It says, "Stranger . . . as you pass by . . ."

SHE

(Disappointed, whispering)
It's gone.

HE

"Reflect . . . that someday you will lie."

SIIE

(Whispering. An urgency)
It's gone. The stone is worn away.

HE

"Here lies Beau . . ."

SHE

(Whispering. More urgent)
It's gone.

183

HE

"Born crippled, died crippled . . . his life in a chair."

SHE
(A moan)

HE

Wait. Here's another. It says . . .
(Pause)
"A lesson. THE ROPE. Here lies Wil . . . and only God can forgive him. The quick and the dead."

SHE

It's broken off.
(Thunderclap, rain)

HE

Let's go back. It's raining.

SHE

I'm drenched!
(Long pause. WILKINSON coughs politely. Stops. Pause.)

TOGETHER
(Each urgent to speak first)
He didn't read mine!
(Sounds recede to normal. Rain continues. Pontifically.)

WILKINSON

The stones have shifted.

BEAU BEAU

Oh, yes?

WILKINSON

Oh yes.

BEAU BEAU
(Quickly, not to be outdone)
Mine toppled long ago.

184

WILKINSON
Oh, yes?

BEAU BEAU
Oh yes.
(Pause. Earnestly)
Wilkinson.
(Pause)
Who are the quick?

WILKINSON
We are.
(Pause)

BEAU BEAU
Wilkinson. Who . . . are the dead?

WILKINSON
We are.
(Pause.)

BEAU BEAU
(Serious, earnest)
Willy. *What's* the difference?

WILKINSON
(A thick, weary laugh. Pause)

BEAU BEAU
Side by side A lump of mud between us, we subtract away.
You know . . . I've never seen your face. Centuries. Eons.
(Emphatically)
The stones *have* moved, toppled. THEY DID!
(Whisper, barely audible)
I've never seen your face . . .
(Sudden, violent)
You must be an ugly sonofabitch!

(The player piano careens into the same tune at once, loud, raucous, fast with the rasping brittle laughter of a woman. Her words convulse out between fits of laughter.)

THE WOMAN WHO HAD NO SHADOW

I HAVE LEGS! I HAVE MY LEGS AND MY ARSE AND WHAT GOES WITH IT ALL IN PLACE, YOU FOOL! Beau Beau. The lover. The crippled pimp who never, NO NEVER, stood up for two centuries. Ask me! Ask the bitch who didn't have a shadow, he says. A pimp who never touched a woman. Beau Beau, who watched and peeped and WHEELED himself into the toilet to live it all over again . . .

(With utter contempt)

. . . behind the door.

(A final burst of laughter. It fades slowly with the player piano music. As it fades into silence, martial drums ascend smartly, nearer, more present, and build to a loud, deafening, compelling crescendo. Ends abruptly. Dead silence.

The wail of a bosun's whistle. 5 seconds. Pause. A clipped, deep voice: alternatingly a chant and rapidly clipped delivery. The chant portion follows the dirge rhythm of the whistle.)

THE MILITARY COMMANDER

GUNNNNNNNNNNNELS GOOOOONNNNNNNE. WE, AT FIRST MARK AND THE STINK OF SULPHUR FAIR TO SNUFF US AAAAaaaaaaaaaAAAAL!

(Neat, precise)

Flying jib to spankER. Full UP. Sounding line a hair to first MARK. Put up another leg-of-mutton 'n SPRITS!

(Ponderous, oratorical)

Here lies in full military honors. OUR HERO! Flogged and beaten, dragged up the hill, rolled down it, drawn and quartered, salted and then smoked . . .

(Soft, celestial)

to preserve him for a better life in the hereafter.
(Proud, beefy)
DECORATED and redecorated.
(Then flippantly, matter-of-fact)
Decorated like a street tart.
(Pause)
The rope still rotting around his neck. And . . . it claimed
the sneaky bastard's life.
(A weary sigh of finality)
He was a traitor.
(Coughs, clears throat commandingly)
MOOOOVE . . . *OUT*!
*(Martial drums crash at once smartly. 10 seconds. They fade
away. Silence except for the rain and the sea. The rain beats
much louder than the sea now.)*

WILKINSON
Steady . . . they're wobbling.

TOGETHER
Steady . . . *steady.*

BEAU BEAU
*(With growing excitement and a reminder of an inescapable
fact)*
The rain, Willy. A soggy bog over here on my side. This old
box, she's rocking something fierce!
(Harder the rain. Thunder)

WILKINSON
"The moon goes by in a pine tree. Now the pine tree comes
in a wagon, dead and soundless."

BEAU BEAU
(Exuberantly)
That's fine. But my wagon's shipping out.
(Shouts)
I hope you built her well, honey. I want it to sail me clear

around the world and back. Land me on a beach where
some pretty thing sits under a parasol reading sonnets.
(Exaggeratedly suspenseful whisper)
She'll tiptoe over and lift the lid care . . . fully. BANG!
I'll clack my teeth and pop my Johnny up at her!
(They laugh. BEAU BEAU'S *fades into the distance. The rain
and the roar of the sea with* WILKINSON'S *hollow laugh left
suspended. It turns into a fit of coughing. The balls have
swung so that the tips of their transits are already offstage.)*

WILKINSON

Scare the hell out of her. Clack your teeth and pop . . .
Beau?
(Pause)
BEAU?!

BEAU BEAU
(From a distance)
Still here. But not for long. I'm shipping out.
(Sings)
> Oh, I know a girl from Bango City,
> She strikes matches on her titty.

*(Player piano very faint. The transits are only half on-stage
at each swing now.)*

WILKINSON

BEAU!
(Music ends. One ball disappears. Softly)
Beau?
(Pause)
Clack your teeth . . .
(Sighs)
"Unknown white hands are caressing our lives." Are they?
From locked keep to locked keep, a length of blackened box
a century. A prison world. He's shipped out. And me?

When? When? With full military honors? WITH FULL
MILITARY HONORS!
   (Drums from the distance approach softly)
With flags waving. Flanks and flanks at attention. Lined up
at the salute. Banners at half mast.
   (Drums recede)
I'll slip out . . . down the bank . . . out on the crests.
   *(Drums out. Rain out. Lights fading. Only the top of the
   ball visible now. A deep sigh. Pause)*
Steady . . . *steady.*
   (Black. Bell buoy. Sea continues to breathe into silence)

CURTAIN

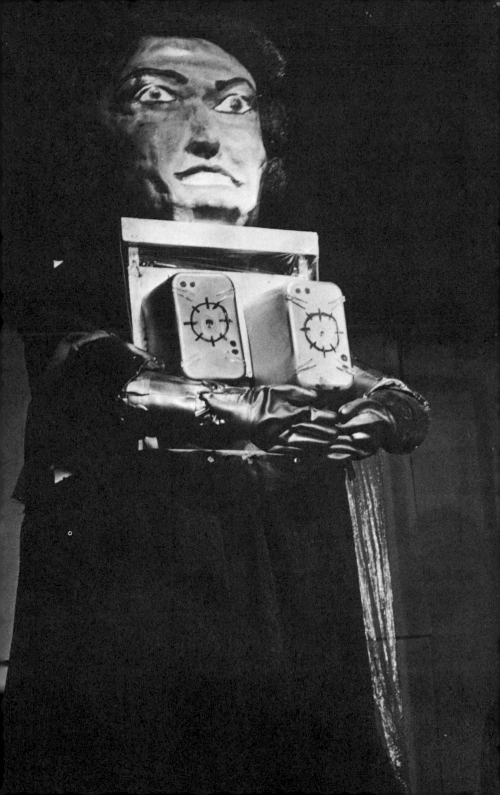

America Hurrah

by Jean-Claude van Itallie

AMERICA HURRAH had its première at the La Mama Experimental Theatre Club on April 28, 1965. It was directed by Michael Kahn with the following cast:

MOTEL-KEEPER DOLL ————————————Cheryl Kilgren

MAN DOLL ——————————————————John Mintun

WOMAN DOLL ————————————————Fay Chaiken

MOTEL-KEEPER'S VOICE————————————Heidi Zimmerli

The design was by Robert Wilson, dolls' bodies were created by Tania Leontov. Music was by Jean Jacques Perret and lighting by John Dodd.

JEAN-CLAUDE VAN ITALLIE *was born in Brussels in 1936. He was raised in Great Neck, Long Island, and graduated from Harvard in 1958. He now lives in Greenwich Village but spends as much time as possible on a farm in Charlemont, Massachusetts. His plays* America Hurrah, War, Almost Like Being, I'm Really Here, The Hunter and the Bird, Pavane, *and* Where Is de Queen *have been performed in New York City by the Open Theatre, at the Cafe La Mama, the Caffe Cino, the Barr-Albee-Wilder Playwrights' Unit, and at the Actors Studio. They have also been performed in Paris and in Copenhagen, at the Academy Theatre in Atlanta, by the Firehouse Theatre in Minneapolis (under the auspices of the Rockefeller Foundation), and on Channel 13 television. For money van Itallie writes public affairs scripts for the television networks.*

America Hurrah

a masque for three dolls

by Jean-Claude van Itallie

*". . . after all our subtle colour and nervous
rhythm, after the faint mixed tints of Conder,
what more is possible? After us the Savage God."*
                                                    Yeats

*(Light will come upon the room very slowly. It will increase
in whiteness to the point of fluorescent glare by the time the
dolls enter.*

*During this dawning a woman's voice will be heard, com-
ing from any place in the theatre, and not necessarily from
any one place continually. The voice will at first be mellow,
mellow and husky. As the light grows harsher and brighter
so the voice will grow older, more set in its pattern, hard
finally, and patronizing and petty.)*

WOMAN'S VOICE

I am an old idea. Gaia I have been, and Lilith. I am an old
idea. Lilly, Molly, Gaia; the walls of the stream that from
which it springs forth. The nothing they enclose with walls,
making then a place from which it springs forth, in which it
happens, in which they happen too. I am that idea: the
place, the walls, the room. A Roman theatre: roofless stone
place where the heat of the sun and the cheers of the people
break loose the fangs of the lion. There was that room too,
a railroad carriage in the Forest of Compiègne, in 1918 and
again in 1941. There have been rooms of marble and rooms

of cork, all letting forth an avalanche. Rooms of mud, rooms of silk. Within which they happen. There is another room here. And it too will be slashed as if by a scimitar, its balconies shuddered, its contents spewed and yawned out. What walls it has will be unsquared, the room tumbriled, its cornices broken. That is what happens. It is almost happening in fact. This is my room too. I made it. I am this room. It's a nice room, not so fancy as some, but with all the conveniences. And a touch of home. The antimacassar comes from my mother's house in Boise. Boise, Idaho. Sits kind of nice, I think, on the Swedish swing. That's my own idea you know. All modern, up to date, that's it—no motel on this route is more up to date. Or cleaner. Go look, then talk me a thing or two. All modern here, but, as I say, with the tang of home. Do you understand? When folks are fatigued, in a strange place? Not that it's old fashioned. No. Not in the wrong way. There's a button-push here for TV. The toilet flushes of its own accord. All you've got to do is get off. Pardon my mentioning it, but you'll have to go far before you see a thing like that on this route. Oh it's quite a room. Yes. And reasonable. Sign here. Pardon the pen leak. I can see you're fatigued. Any children? Well, that's nice. Children don't appreciate travel. And rooms don't appreciate children. As it happens it's the last one I've got left. I'll just flip my vacancy switch. Twelve dollars please. In advance that'll be. That way you can go any time you want to go, you know, get an early start. On a trip to see sights, are you? That's nice. You just get your luggage while I go unlock the room. You can see the light.

(The MOTEL-KEEPER *enters through the door. It is a large doll, slightly larger than human size, though not a giantess. The dancers will be inside the dolls. Their movements will have the quality of ritual, their fascination will be that of a dance or a machine: strictly controllable, humorous some-*

times, but increasingly violent and disturbing. The MOTEL-
KEEPER *doll is predominantly gray, feminine, with square
breasts and a triangular skirt. On its mask it wears large
square eyeglasses which are mirrors. It doesn't matter what
these mirrors reflect at any given moment. The audience may
occasionally catch a glimpse of itself, or be bothered by re-
flections of light. It doesn't matter; the sensory nerves of the
audience are not to be spared. It may be more feasible for
the* MOTEL-KEEPER'S *voice to continue coming from a loud-
speaker, with accompanying rhythmic jaw motions on the
part of the doll.)*

MOTEL-KEEPER'S VOICE

There now. What I say doesn't matter. You can see. It
speaks for itself. The room speaks for itself. You can see it's
a perfect 1966 room. But a taste of home. I've seen to that. A
taste of home.

(She turns down the covers on the double bed.)

Comfy, cozy, nice, but a taste of newness. That's what. You
can see it.

(She snaps up the shades. There are neon lights outside.)

The best stop on route six sixty-six. Well, there might be
others like it, but this is the best stop. You've arrived at the
right place. This place. And a hooked rug. I don't care
what but I've said no room is without a hooked rug.

(She centers the rug.)

No complaints yet. Never.

(The WOMAN *doll enters. It is the same size as the* MOTEL-
KEEPER. *Its shoulders are thrown way back, like a girl pos-
ing for a calendar ad. Its breasts are wiggleable. It has glam-
orous blonde hair and a cherry-lipstick smile. Its clothes, real
clothes these, are those of a young married woman. The*
WOMAN *doll goes directly to the bathroom and doesn't shut
the door. There is absolutely no rapport between the other*

195

dolls and the MOTEL-KEEPER. *The other dolls do not ever stop what they are doing, and they are perpetually doing something. The* MOTEL-KEEPER *is sometimes still and sometimes ambulates in circles. But all her remarks are directed generally; she is never motivated by the actions of other dolls.)*

Modern people like modern places. Oh yes. I can tell. They tell me. And reasonable. Very very reasonable rates. No cheaper rates on the route, not for this. You receive what you pay for.

(The toilet flushes.)

All that driving and driving and driving. Fatigued. You must be. I would be. Miles and miles and miles.

(The toilet flushes again.)

Fancy. Fancy your ending up right here. You didn't know and I didn't know. But you did. End up right here. Respectable and decent and homelike. Right here.

(The MAN *doll enters carrying suitcases. He is the same size as the others. His clothes are real and vulgar, unremarkable.)*

All folks everywhere sitting in the very palm of God. Waiting, whither, whence.

(The MAN *doll begins an inspection of the bed. The* WOMAN *doll comes rapidly from the bathroom, opens one of the suitcases, and messily rummages for toilet articles with which she returns to the bathroom.)*

Any motel you might have come to on six sixty-six. Any motel. On that vast network of roads. Whizzing by, whizzing by. Trucks too. And cars from everywhere. Full up with folks, all sitting in the very palm of God. I can tell proper folks when I get a look at them. All folks.

(The MAN *doll pulls at the coverlet in every direction, testing its strength. He begins to jump on every part of the mattress.)*

Country roads, state roads, United States roads. It's a big

world and here you are. I noticed you got a license plate.
I've not been to there myself. I've not been to anywhere
myself, excepting Town for supplies, and Boise. Boise,
Idaho.

(The MAN *doll is now jumping heavily on the mattress.)*

The world arrives to me, you'd say. It's a small world. These
plastic flowers here: "Made in Japan" on the label. You
noticed? Got them from the catalogue. Cat-a-logue. Every
product in this room is ordered.

(Pieces of the WOMAN *doll's clothing are thrown from the
bathroom.)*

Ordered from the catalogue. Excepting the antimacassar
and the hooked rug. Made the hooked rug myself. Tang of
home. No room is a room without. Course the bedspread,
hand-hooked, hooked near here at Town. Mrs. Harritt.
Betsy Harritt gets materials through another catalogue.
Cat-a-logue.

*(Now toilet articles and fixtures from the bathroom follow
the clothing.*

The WOMAN *doll returns, without clothes. She applies
more lipstick to her lips and nipples—her breasts are ob-
scenely huge. The* MAN *doll takes off his trousers.)*

Myself, I know it from the catalogue: bottles, bras, break-
fasts, refrigerators, cast-iron gates, plastic posies, paper sub-
scriptions, Buick trucks, blankets, forks, clitter-clack darn-
ing hooks, transistors and antimacassars, vinyl plastics,

(The WOMAN *doll blots her lipstick on the walls. The* MAN
doll strikes at objects in the room with a cigar.)

crazy quilts, paper hairpins, cats, catnip, club feet, canisters,
bannisters, holy books, tattooed toilet articles, tables, tea-
cozies,

(On the wall the MAN *doll writes simple obscenities with his
cigar. She does the same with her lipstick.)*

pickles, bayberry candles, South Dakotan kewpie dolls, fiberglas hair, polished milk, amiable grandpappies, colts, Galsworthy books, cribs, cabinets, teeter-totters,

(The MAN *and* WOMAN *dolls have turned to picture-making. They work together; he with his cigar, her filling in with her lipstick.)*

and television sets.

(The MOTEL-KEEPER *doll turns on the television set which eventually starts glaring.)*

Oh I tell you it, I do. It's a wonder. Full with things, the world, full up. Shall I tell you my thought? Next year there's a shelter to be built by me, yes. Shelter motel. Everything to be placed under the ground. Signs up in every direction up and down six sixty-six. "Complete Security," "Security While You Sleep Tight," "Bury Your Troubles at This Motel," "Homelike, Very Comfy, and Encased in Lead," "Every Room Its Own Set," "Fourteen Day Emergency Supplies $5.00 Extra,"

(The MAN *doll pushes the TV button with his cigar, and the TV plays the twist. The* MAN *and* WOMAN *dolls twist.)*

"Self-Contained Latrine Waters," "Filters, Counters, Periscopes and Mechanical Doves," "Hooked Rugs," "Dearest Little Picture Frames for Loved Ones (Made in Japan)," through the catalogue. Cat-a-logue. You can pick items and products: cablecackles (so nice), cuticles, twice-twisted combs with corrugated calesthenics, meat-beaters, fish-tackles, bug bombs,

(The MOTEL-KEEPER'S *voice is slowly drowned out by the twist music. The* MAN *and* WOMAN *dolls, moving ever more rapidly, tear the bedspread in two, tear the rug, and smash the framed prints on the wall. A civil defense siren's noise starts to build up.)*

toasted terra-cotta'd Tanganyikan switch blades, ocher closets, ping pong balls, didies, capricorn and cancer prognostics, crackers, total uppers, stickpins, basting tacks . . .

198

(As the two dolls continue to destroy they dismantle the MOTEL-KEEPER *doll, tear down the curtains, and finally start to rip apart the walls. The civil defense siren comes up to full pitch. Each of the dolls' movements must be choreographed, with nothing left haphazard. There is no disorder in what they do, only increasingly violent destruction.*

Suddenly all noise and movement will cease. Against a dark backdrop the audience will contemplate, for five or six seconds, an available object of incredible beauty, possibly a rear-projection slice of a quiet painting by Vermeer.

The curtain call should be taken by the dancers without their masks and dolls. Preferably a fourth person—director, stage manager, anyone—should appear too.)

THE END

THE OPEN THEATRE

JOSEPH CHAIKIN, actor, founder, and co-director with Peter Feldman of the Open Theatre.

The Open Theatre is a group of actors, playwrights, directors, painters, musicians, and critics who come together in laboratory—the actors to build on their work in ensemble and all of us to collaborate jointly in developing and experimenting with new forms in theatre. We have several acting and writing workshops and give limited public performances. This past season Ellen Stewart has made Cafe La Mama available to us for a production each month. Together in the last three years we have presented about twenty programs—plays, improvisations, and pieces constructed in collaboration by the company. In addition we have performed the works of John Arden, T. S. Eliot, and Bertolt Brecht.

Most of our work is structured around the acting ensemble. We are responsible for presenting the works of the Open Theatre playwrights: Maria Irene Fornes, Sam Shepard, Michael Smith, Megan Terry, Sharon Thie, and Jean-Claude van Itallie, each of whom has a different relationship to the Open Theatre and uses its workshops in a different way. Jean-Claude van Itallie and Megan Terry, since first beginning with us as playwrights, have been most important in forming theatre pieces from the group's exercises and improvisations.

Theatre is the collaborative art. But often the director gets in the way of the actors, the actors in each other's way, the playwright in the way of the play. Yet finally it is all intended for a single event. We continue to work toward a dialogue between the artists, in terms both of discussion and of exercises. The plays as well as the exercises are about many different things.

At the Open Theatre we are not trying to groom ourselves for the current business theatre, but to explore and experiment. In the workshops we project questions through stage exercises and improvisations. Recently we have been exploring extensions of the audience/performer relationship. Something which we continually come back to is the impulse behind the useless war this country is fighting and the condition of peril we live in, with nations pointing prepared nuclear weapons at each other. Can these larger issues be seen in personal, one-to-one relationships? We are trying to use the theatre to make visible the human situation at a time when "things could be different." But only some of the work and thought is in social terms. Much of the work is abstract and nonliteral. When we begin on a new form or idea, we have no way of knowing if it will result in anything visible or lend any clarity. Often it doesn't.

When you take a job in the theatre, you must become the size and shape of that job. At the Open Theatre we have the feeling that this is not enough. It is not possible to make discoveries under the pressure to please, to gain audiences and money. Only in a climate where people are listening to their own drumbeats can it be possible. It is then necessary to close off this impulse to "make it" in order to open oneself to other voices.

The structure and emphasis of attention of the Open Theatre is always changing. I have no idea what will happen in the future.

The Successful Life of 3

a skit for vaudeville

by Maria Irene Fornes

THE SUCCESSFUL LIFE OF 3 was presented at the Sheridan Square Playhouse in March 1965 for a single performance. Joseph Chaikin directed the first production. The play was redirected by Richard Gilman and performed again a month later. The cast for both productions was as follows:

3————————————————————Paul Boesing
HE————————————————————James Barbosa
SHE————————————————————Barbara Vann
BODYGUARDS AND POLICEMEN————Sydney Schubert Walter,
Ron Faber, Rhea Gaisner

The play was first produced by the Firehouse Theatre in Minneapolis, Minnesota, under a Rockefeller Foundation program administered by the Office for Advanced Drama Research of the University of Minnesota.

MARIA IRENE FORNES *was born in Havana, Cuba, in 1930. She came to the United States in 1945 and started painting in 1949. She lived in Paris from 1954 to 1957 and began writing plays in 1960, after returning to New York. Her first play,* The Widow, *was published in Spanish and performed on the radio by the University of Mexico. She received a John Hay Whitney Fellowship in 1961 and wrote* Tango Palace, *which has been produced in San Francisco, Spoleto, Minneapolis, and in the workshops of the Actors Studio and IASTA in New York.* The Successful Life of 3 *was produced by the Firehouse Theatre in Minneapolis and the Open Theatre in New York. Her musical* Promenade, *with music by Al Carmines, was presented by the Judson Poets' Theatre in 1965. She won the "Obie" Award for Distinguished Playwriting in 1964–65 for* Promenade *and* The Successful Life of 3.

The Successful Life of 3

a skit for vaudeville

by Maria Irene Fornes

To Susan Sontag

CHARACTERS: 3, *a plump, middle-aged man.* HE, *a handsome young man.* SHE, *a sexy young lady.* BODYGUARDS *and* POLICE-MEN

*(When "*SHE*" is followed by asterisks,* SHE *thinks with a stupid expression. The others watch her.*

*When "*HE*" is followed by asterisks,* HE *looks disdainful. The others watch him.*

When "3" is followed by asterisks, 3 looks with intense curiosity. The others watch him.

Very deadpan.)

SCENE 1

(The Doctor's Office. 3 and HE *sit.* HE *is combing his hair. 3 takes a shoe off and drops it. At the sound of the shoe,* HE *becomes motionless, his arms suspended in the air. 3 looks at* HE *and freezes for a moment.)*

3

What are you doing?

HE

Waiting.

3

What for?

HE

For the other shoe to drop.

3

Ah, and I was wondering what you were doing. If I hadn't asked, we would have stayed like that forever. You waiting and me wondering . . . That's the kind of person I am. I ask . . . That's good, you know.

HE

Why?

3

* * *

HE

Why?

3

It starts action.

HE

What action did you start?

3

We're talking.

HE

That's nothing. We could as well be waiting for the shoe to drop.
(HE *suspends his arms in the air again.* 3 *stares at* HE. *They remain motionless for a while.*)

3

Sorry . . . I'm going to do my sewing.

HE

First take the other shoe off. Get it over with.

208

3
(Taking his shoe off)
I wasn't going to take it off.
(3 takes needle and thread and sews a button on his shirt.)
You see? If I do it now I don't have to do it later.

HE
What?

3
The sewing.

HE
And what are you going to do later?

3
* * *
(3 puts the needle and thread away.)
Look, there are advantages to being optimistic.

HE
Sure.

3
What are they?

HE
You tell me.

3
Well, it makes one feel happier.

HE
You don't look happy to me.

3
Oh, no?

HE
No.

3

Well, things are not what they appear to the eye.

HE

They aren't?

3

Are they?

HE

Sometimes . . . sometimes they are just what they appear to
the eye. . . . Don't generalize.

3

Why?

HE

Because there are always exceptions. There's always one
that isn't like the others.

3

If it's just one, it can be thrown in with the rest. It doesn't
matter.

HE

It matters.

3

Perhaps you can exclude it in your mind. Without mentioning it.

HE

You have to mention it. . . . You're splitting hairs anyway.

3

I like splitting hairs.

HE

Well, do it when I'm not around.

3
I was just joking.

HE
(*Correcting him*)
Being facetious.
(*3 takes an apple from his pocket.*)

3
Want an apple?

HE
No.

3
An apple a day keeps the doctor away.

HE
I knew you were going to say that.
(SHE *enters wearing a nurse's uniform.*)
Miss, you're a fine dish.

SHE
Thanks.
(SHE *exits and re-enters.*)

HE
Miss, I would like to bounce on you.

SHE
Thank you.
(*To 3*)
Come in, please.
(*3 and* SHE *exit.* SHE *re-enters.*)

HE
Miss, I would like to bang you.

SHE

Your friend just did.

HE

Well, I'm next.

SHE

I only do it once a day.

HE

I get you all worked up and you do it with him instead?

SHE

* * *

HE

I'm handsome and sexy and I get you all worked up, and you go and do it with him? . . . Answer now.

SHE

What?

HE

Is that natural?

SHE

I don't know.
  (3 enters.)

HE

A moment ago I was thinking of marrying you.

SHE

You just saw me for the first time.

3

He figured he'd see you a few more times if he married you.

HE

Don't speak for me after you ruined everything. . . . Let me try again. Miss, would you go to the movies with me after work?

SHE

Okay, I like the movies.

HE

Everybody likes the movies.

SHE

I never liked them until a few months ago.

HE

What made you like them then?

SHE

I saw a movie with the Lane sisters.

HE

You like them?

SHE

Yes, they're all right.

HE

What do they do?

SHE

Stupid things.

HE

Like what?

SHE

They cry and laugh.

HE

That doesn't sound so great.

SHE

I like it. It's all right if you like sisters.

3

I like movies about marriage, divorce, and remarriage.

SHE

I like sisters.

HE

I don't have any particular preference. I just like good movies . . . with action and a lot of killing.

SHE

I couldn't go to the movies if I didn't have a preference.

3

Neither could I.
(3 takes SHE *by the hand and exits.* SHE *re-enters.)*

HE

Did you make it with him again?

SHE

Yes.

HE

How long are you going to keep this up?

SHE

I don't know.
(3 re-enters.)

HE

Listen, I was even thinking of marrying you.

SHE

You'd have to give me a ring for that. Two rings. An en-
gagement ring and a wedding band.

3

I'll give the bride away.

214

HE

From the looks of it you're not leaving anything to give away.

3

And I'm not through yet.

HE

I didn't say you were.

3

You didn't say I was but you sure wish I were.

SHE

Me too.

HE

I never wish.

SHE

In my profession you have to wish.

3

For what?

SHE

* * *

HE

I don't have a profession.

SHE

How are you going to support me?

HE

I'll find a way.

3

He sure does have to support you. Doesn't he?

SHE

Yeah, my parents pay for the wedding and he supports me.

3

I'll pay for the wedding.

HE

He doesn't have any money. Get your parents to pay for the wedding.

SHE

Weddings are a pain in the neck.

3

Why do you want one then?

SHE

* * *

HE

Don't you see she doesn't know?

3

Yes, I see.

SHE

The Andrews sisters are all married.

HE

Do you like brothers too?

SHE

Not so much.

HE

Did you see the Corsican Brothers?

SHE

That's not brothers. That's just Douglas Fairbanks playing twins. It's not the same.

216

HE
What brothers do you like?

SHE
I don't know any.

HE
How do you know you like them?

SHE
* * *

3
She didn't say she liked them.

HE
Didn't you say you liked them?

SHE
No, I said, "Not so much." . . . I don't think I'm going to marry you.

3
Why?

HE
I can ask my own questions, if you please.
(*To* SHE)
Why?

SHE
You're too picky.

HE
That's all right. Are we going to the movies or not?

SHE
Sure.

3

If you find a sister movie.

SHE

That's all right. I'll try another kind.

3

Let's go in for a quickie before you leave.
(3 and SHE *exit.* SHE *re-enters wearing a hat.)*

HE

Ready?

SHE

Yes.

HE

Hey, didn't you say you only do it once a day?

SHE

Yes.

HE

How come you did it with him three times already?

SHE

* * *

HE

You're not a liar, are you?

SHE

No.

HE

You better not be, because I can't stand liars.
(3 re-enters. HE *and* SHE *exit.)*

3

Wait for me.
(3 exits.)

SCENE 2

(The Movies. A few minutes later. The lights go down and flicker. HE, *3, and* SHE *enter. They sit—3 in the middle,* SHE *and* HE *at his sides.)*

HE

Hey, what do you mean by sitting next to her? Change with me. She's my date.

3

I can't feel her up from there.

HE

You don't have to feel her up.
   (3 and HE *change seats.)*

3

How about some popcorn?

SHE

I'll go.

3

Don't go. Let him go.

HE

You go.

3

I'm tired.
   *(*HE *exits. 3 moves next to* SHE. HE *re-enters.)*

HE

Move back to your seat.

3

I already moved once. I'm not moving twice. Let's have some popcorn.
   *(*HE *offers popcorn to 3.)*

I'll hold it because I'm in the middle.
  (3 *tries to hold the bag, eat popcorn, and feel* SHE *up.*)
You hold the bag. I can't feel her up and eat at the same
time if I hold the bag.
  (HE *takes the bag.*)

HE
At least wait till the feature starts.

SCENE 3

  (*The Porch. Ten years later.* HE *dozes.* SHE *peels potatoes.* 3
  sews.)

SHE
I'm going to divorce him.

3
Give him another chance.

SHE
Him?

3
He's not bad.

SHE
Yes, he is.

3
There are worse.

SHE
No, there aren't.

3
Wouldn't it be worse if you were married to me?

SHE

What difference would it make?

3

It would make a difference.

SHE

No, it wouldn't.

3

Yes, it would.

SHE

What difference?

3

* * *

SHE

What difference?

3

I'll ask him.

(3 shakes HE.)

Hey, would it make any difference if she was married to me instead of you?

HE

Yeah.

3

What difference?

HE

Ask her. She ought to know.

3

She doesn't know.

HE

She never knows anything.

3

Actually, this time she knows. She said it wouldn't make any difference.

HE

She's probably right, because she usually doesn't know anything.

SHE

I'm going to divorce him whether I'm right or wrong.

3

Marry a worse one for a while . . . then remarry him and you'll be happier.

HE

That would be like wearing tight shoes so it feels better when you take them off.

3

That's the idea. Do it.

SHE

You can't do that.

3

Why not?

SHE

I don't know.

3
(*To* HE)

Do you know why you can't wear tight shoes so it feels better when you take them off?

HE

No.

SHE

But isn't it true that you're not supposed to?

HE

Yeah.

SHE

I knew it.

3

Well, you'd be happier if you did it.

SHE

You're not supposed to.

HE

(To 3)

Get off that chair. I want to put my feet up.
(3 moves to another chair.)

3

Rivalry.

SHE

What?

3

Rivalry.

SHE

* * *

3

Masculine rivalry.

SHE

* * *

3

Masculine rivalry.
(3 points to HE *and to himself.)*

SHE

Who ever heard of such a thing.

3
What?

SHE
What you said.

3
Rivalry?

SHE
Yeah.

3
You haven't heard of it?

SHE
No.

3
I bet you he has.
   (To HE*)*
Have you heard of rivalry?

HE
Sure.

3
See?

SHE
I mean the other.

3
Masculine?

SHE
Both, both together.

3
   (To HE*)*
Have you heard of masculine rivalry?

HE
Yeah.

SHE
So he has.
(*3 looks* SHE *over.*)

3
I don't desire you any more.

SHE
Thank God.

3
Don't thank God. Thank me.

SHE
Stop picking on me.

HE
Are you picking on her again?

3
I can't help it.

HE
Stop picking on her.

3
Masculine rivalry.

HE
What are you talking about? There's no comparison. I'm sexy and you're slimy.

SHE
That's the only thing I like about him.

HE
You like *that*?

SHE

It's all right. . . . But I'm tired of having children.

HE

That's not true. You told me you like children.

SHE

Not that many.

3

How many are there?

SHE

I don't know.

3

How do you know there are too many?

SHE

* * *

3

I'll go count them.
(3 exits.)

HE

Listen, you can't one day say you like babies and the next day say you don't.

SHE

Why not?

HE

You have to make up your mind.

SHE

* * *

HE

Well?

226

SHE
I can't stand the twins.

HE
Why not?

SHE
They look too much alike.

HE
Twins always do.

SHE
I didn't say they didn't.

HE
You didn't say they did either.

SHE
No, all I said was that I didn't like them.

HE
Why?

SHE
I don't see why they have to dress alike.

HE
Twins always do.

SHE
I didn't say they didn't.

HE
Bring the food out.

SHE
There's no food.

HE
How come?

SHE

You know how come.

HE

No, I don't.

SHE

You're supposed to provide for me, but you don't.

HE

Don't I get you all the potatoes?

SHE

I'm going, I can't stand peeling potatoes all the time.
(SHE *exits.* 3 *enters.*)

HE

She left.

3

Oh.

HE

That's all right. I never want what I don't have.

3

I missed it.

HE

What?

3

Her leaving.

HE

* * *

3

I've been waiting around to see her leave, and now she does
it when I'm not looking. How did she go?

HE
* * *

SCENE 4

(The Porch. Three years later. HE *peels potatoes.* 3 *sews.)*

3

I'm going into business. I can't stand this home life any longer.

HE

You wouldn't be any good at it.

3

I might as well try it.

HE

You would just lose all your money.

3

I don't have any money.

HE

How're you going to go into business?

3

I'll put a bid on some nylon rope, go South, convince the fishermen to use nylon instead of whatever they use, and take them for all they've got.

HE

They probably use nylon.

3

Then I'll sell it to them cheap and still make a fortune.

HE

It wouldn't work.

3

No? . . . Well, I can make a sandwich with peanut butter and Ritz crackers, dip it in chocolate, call it Tootsie Tootsie, and sell it.

HE

You're better off with the nylon rope.

3

I thought so too. I'll go try it.

HE

Okay.

3

Goodbye. Give my love to Ruth if you see her. Have you seen her?

HE

Yes, she's happily married.

3

Who to?

HE

I don't know.

3

Well, if you see her tell her I would still like a roll in the hay with her, even if she's getting old and decrepit.

HE

Okay, I'll tell her.

3

Goodbye. You do think it will work.

HE

Sure.

3

Goodbye then.

(*3 exits.*)

HE

Just said that to get rid of him.

(*3 re-enters wearing top hat and furs.*)

3

It worked.

HE

Don't tell me it worked.

3

(*Respectfully*)

Oh, sorry.

HE

What do you mean it worked?

3

I put a bid on some nylon rope, went South, convinced the fishermen to use nylon instead of whatever they were using, and took them for all they had. D'you know rope is sold by the weight, not the measure?

HE

Don't get smart with me, Arthur. I'm very annoyed. I have all the brains and the looks and it's you who goes South with your squeaky voice and sweaty hands and makes all the money.

3

And I'm not finished yet. I'm going to make that peanut butter sandwich and make another mint.

HE

You're making me sick.

3

Don't get sick yet. I'm just starting. You think Ruth likes
money?

HE

Sure.

3

Perhaps she'll come live with us for the money. It'll be good
for the children.

HE

I'm the husband and the father. I'll make my own decisions.

3

Yeah, but I do all the screwing and make all the money.

HE

Don't rub it in.

3

Sorry.

HE

You may make all the money and all that but you have no
manners.

3

Teach me manners.
   (HE *puts on a top hat and furs.* SHE *enters.*)

SHE

Okay, I came back.

HE

Because of the money.

SHE

I like money.

HE

Everybody likes money. You say it as if it was something special.

SHE

It is special. I like money very much.

3

More than sisters?

SHE

* * *

HE

Never mind.

3

I have a present for you.
 (3 gives SHE *three men's hats.)*

SHE

These are men's hats. What's the matter with you?

3

Nothing.

HE

He doesn't know his ass from his elbow.

3

I do.
 (3 points to his buttocks and his elbow.)
I only didn't know what kind of hat to buy.

SHE

Where's the money.

3

In the bank.

SHE

Oh, damn it. I came for the money and you put it away.

HE

You didn't come for that. You didn't come for that. You came for me and for the children.

SHE

You said I came for the money.

HE

I was just accusing you.

SHE

And what was I supposed to say?

HE

"I didn't. I didn't. I came for you and the children." Defend yourself.

SHE

Well, I didn't.

HE

I don't have to stay here while you come back for his money. I'm sexy and bright and you're a bunch of morons. I'm leaving.
(3 puts his arm around SHE.*)*
You don't have to jump on her the moment I turn my back.
(3 lets go of SHE*)*

SHE

I'm glad he caught you.

HE

You can do what you want. I'm leaving. Goodbye.
*(*HE *exits.)*

SHE

What are we going to do without him?

3

Wait for him.

SCENE 5

(The Store. Three years later. 3 steals a pipe. HE *enters.)*

HE

Arthur!

3

What are you doing here?

HE

I'm a store detective.

3

How long have you been a store detective?

HE

Since I left the house.

3

Is the pay good?

HE

Not for the risk you take.

3

What risk?

HE

You might get hit or knifed.

3

Who would do that?

HE

The thief. You see, I grab him like this. I identify myself and I tell him to go with me to the office. Then he either becomes frightened and comes along quietly, or becomes violent and attacks me.

(3 punches HE *and runs.)*

SCENE 6

(The Porch. A few minutes later. SHE *peels potatoes.* 3 *enters smoking the pipe.)*

3

I just saw him. He's a detective.

SHE

I don't like detectives.

3

Why?

SHE

I can't understand them.

3

Why not?

SHE

They talk too fast.

3

He's a store detective. They don't talk fast.

SHE

A store detective is not a real detective.

3

Someone stole something though.

SHE

Did he figure out who did it?

3

I don't know. I hit him and ran.

SHE

You didn't run so fast. You're late for dinner. . . . Did you figure out who did it?

3

Yeah, I did it.

SHE

What did you do?

3

(Showing her the pipe)

Stole it.

(HE enters.)

HE

Why did you hit me?

SHE

Is that a way to come in after you've been gone for three years? Can't you say hello?

HE

I don't feel like saying hello.

SHE

You could at least pretend.

HE

Why did you hit me?

3

Because I had to.

HE

Why?

3

Because I'm the thief and you're the detective.

HE

What did you steal?

3

Guess.

HE

I give up.

3

The pipe.

HE

Now I have to take you in.

3

You have to identify yourself.

HE

Don't be silly. You know me. Come on.

3

Goodbye, Ruth.

SHE

Goodbye.

SCENE 7

(The Porch. Three days later. SHE *and* HE *are sitting.)*

SHE

How come you came back now?

HE

Because he's away. . . . Masculine rivalry.

SHE

That's what he always says.

HE

So what. It's true.

SHE

How come he was stealing?

HE

He didn't know he could take the money out of the bank.

SHE

Can he?

HE

Yeah.

(3 enters wearing a prisoner's uniform.)

3

I organized a revolt and got out.

HE

Can't you stay put in one place?

3

Can't I?

HE

No, you're always jumping from place to place.

3

I'll stay put now. Ruth, even if you're getting old and decrepit, I still want you. Jail makes a man want a woman.

HE

You disgust me. You spend three days in jail and you don't learn anything.

3

I did so. I organized the prisoners and now I'm the head of the mob. If you want I'll make you my bodyguard.

HE

You call that a body?

3

I know. I have to do some exercise. But in the meantime it's all right to call it a body.

HE

It is not all right with me. I'm leaving.

SHE

He's always leaving.

3

Like Shane . . . Stay and have some fun. The guys are coming presently.

HE

What kind of idiot are you that says presently?

3

No idiot. I'm the Alec Guinness type gangster.

HE

God damn it. I'm getting fed up. You have no style, no
looks, you act like an old housewife, and it's you who gets
to jail and becomes the head of the mob.

SHE

Let's eat.

HE

Okay, but if you want me to be your bodyguard, you have
to give me a good salary. . . . No. I don't care if you get
slugged. Goodbye.
(HE *exits*.)

3

You be my bodyguard, Ruth.

SHE

Okay, but I don't move from this chair.

3

You have to move. You have to keep an eye on me.

SHE

Skip it. Who wants to look at you all the time.

3

Okay, don't be my bodyguard. I'll get the guys to look after
me.

SCENE 8

(The Porch. Six months later. 3 and SHE *sit. 3 is armed to the teeth.* BODYGUARDS *surround him.)*

3
I have a sweet streak in me.

SHE
Where?

3
* * *

SHE
What did you say?

3
I have a sweet streak in me.

SHE
Me too.

3
I'm tired of the life of crime.

SHE
Why don't you stop stealing?

3
I like stealing.

SHE
I thought you said you were tired of crime.

3
Yes, but not of stealing.

SHE
You're not supposed to steal.

3

Says who?

SHE

* * *

3

You don't know anything. I'm going to steal from the rich and give to the poor.

SHE

I came back for the money and you're going to give it to the poor? I'm leaving.

3

Where are you going?

SHE

I'll go find a Joan Fontaine movie.

3

What good would that do you?

SHE

She's Olivia de Havilland's sister.

3

No, she's not.

SHE

Yes, she is.

3

They don't look alike.

SHE

The Lane sisters don't look alike either.

3

No, but they act like sisters.

SHE
* * *

3

Go if you want. I'm leaving first.
(SHE *and* 3 *run for the door.*)

SCENE 9

(*The Store. A few minutes later.* HE *is standing.* 3 *walks by surrounded by* BODYGUARDS.)

HE

Come with me to the office. You penny-pinching sonofa-bitch hoodlum. I finally caught you.

3

What for? I just came to get a Zorro costume.
(*3 puts on a Zorro costume.*)

HE

You look like an idiot, like you always did. Did you steal it?

3

I bought it.

HE

Show me the sales slip.

3

I lost it.

HE

You stole it.
(*To the* BODYGUARDS)
Did he steal it?

BODYGUARDS

Yeah.

HE

Come with me.

3

Don't be silly. If I'm Zorro and the store is rich, I have to steal from it. Now I have to give something to the poor. Here's a penny.

HE

I'm turning you in anyway. I'll get fired if I don't catch someone soon. I haven't caught anyone since the last time I caught you. Get moving.

3

No, I won't. I have better things to do, like ride around the pampas with my mask on. Come with me and you can ride too.

HE

What kind of idiot d'you think I am. You'll make me do all the riding and cut all the Z's and you'll get all the credit. You do your own dirty work.

3

No, I won't. . . . I'm getting too old to ride around like an idiot.

HE

You used to do your own dirty work.

3

Yeah. But now I'm rich and lazy.
(*To a* BODYGUARD)
Can you ride?
(*The* BODYGUARD *shakes his head.*)
Can you ride?
(*The* BODYGUARD *shakes his head.*)

Can you ride?
  (The BODYGUARD *shakes his head.)*
Get out of my way. I don't need you any more.
  (To HE*)*
Can Ruth ride?

HE

No, she can't do anything.

3

That's all right. I'll go to some rodeo and get myself a double.
  (3 exits.)

SCENE 10

(The Porch. Three days later HE *sits.* 3 *enters panting.)*

3

Hide me.

HE

What from?

3

I'm being followed.

HE

What did you do?

3

I got tired of stealing from the rich and giving to the poor and started stealing from the rich and the poor. Hide me.

HE

I won't hide you. I don't care if they catch you.

3

Hide my *antifaz* then.

HE

What's that?

3

My mask. Do you know that Zorro means fox in Spanish?

HE

Never mind. I don't care if Zorro means fox. I can't hide your *antifaz*. I'll lose my job if I get caught with stolen goods.

3

I thought they were going to fire you.

HE

I caught a girl who didn't do anything and they let me stay.

3

That's not nice. Where's Ruth?

HE

She went to see Joan Fontaine and never came back.

3

Did she take any money with her?

HE

She doesn't need any money. She married the guy who owns the movie.

3

How're the children?

HE

They're all right. They're always playing doctor.

3

Are they sick?

HE

No, they just play doctor.
(*The* POLICEMEN *enter and grab* 3.)

246

3

Where're you taking me?

POLICEMEN

To the scaffold.

3

Oh! Merciful God.
(*The* POLICEMEN *take* 3 *away.* 3 *re-enters. He carries a bouquet.*)

HE

I thought they were going to hang you.

3

I got out of it. Here's Ruth. She must have broken up with
that movie man.
(SHE *enters.* 3 *gives her the flowers.*)

SHE

How did you know that I was coming?

3

I didn't.

HE

How did you get out?

3

I told them you did it.

HE

I'll lose my job at the store.

3

Don't let that worry you. You won't need a job any more.
They're coming to get you any minute.
(*To* SHE)
What made you come back?

SHE

I'm old and tired and I've had too many men. I'm just going to sit here and rest for the rest of my life.

3

Oh no you don't. You have to work for your keep. Scrub the floor.

HE

I'm going to the store. I can't stand seeing my wife scrubbing floors.

SHE

Don't go. I'm not going to scrub no floors. You've become a mean old sonofabitch, Arthur.

3

I was always mean. I just didn't know it.

SHE

You're not supposed to be mean.

3

Why not?

SHE

* * *

HE

She's right. You're not supposed to be mean.

SHE

I knew it.

3

Well, perhaps I just have a mean streak in me.

SHE

Yeah, like the Grand Canyon.

HE

The Grand Canyon is not a streak.

SHE

What is it?

3

It's a ditch.

SHE

Same thing.

3

Well, here are the cops anyway. They're coming to get you.

HE

You're disgusting. You go around being a sonofabitch and then you pin it on me. What am I going to do now?

3

* * *

SHE

* * *

HE

You're a bunch of morons.

(The POLICEMEN *enter. They grab 3.)*

3

Where are you taking me?

POLICEMEN

To the scaffold.

3

I just came from there.

(The POLICEMEN *take 3 away.)*

SHE

Are you going to miss him?

HE

No, he's a sonofabitch—are you?

SHE

What?

HE

Going to miss him?

SHE

* * *

   (3 enters with a bouquet of flowers and gives them to SHE.)

HE

How come you always come back with flowers?

3

They have them there.

SHE

What for?

3

For the grave.

HE

Did you steal them?

3

No, they give them to you.

SHE

They go bad if they don't use them.

HE

How did you get away this time?

3

They caught the real Zorro.

SHE

I thought you were the real Zorro.

3

No, I'm too young.

HE

Bring in the food, Ruth.

SHE

What food?

3

I have some Tootsie Tootsie.
(They eat Tootsie Tootsies. A POLICEMAN *enters. 3 shoots him dead.)*
I'm not armed to the teeth for nothing.
(They freeze for a moment. Then they sing the "Song to Ignorance.")

SHE, HE, AND 3

> Oh, let me be wrong.
> But also not know it.
> Be wrong
> Be wrong
> And, oh, not to know it.
> Oh! Let me be wrong.

3

> One day while walking
> Down the street,
> I found a petunia
> And took it.
> I took it.
> Oh! Let me be wrong.

SHE

> I went from here
> To I don't know where.
> I don't know where.
>
> I called a parasol an umbrella
> Yes, an umbrella
> Oh, let me be wrong.
> I don't care.

HE

> I sprichen si Dutch very well
> I said to Herr Auber;
> Herr Auber, I sprichen si
> Dutch very well. . . .
> Herr Auber.
> Oh! Let me be wrong.
> Be wrong.

ALL

> Oh! Let me be wrong.
> But also not know it.
> I want to be wrong.

(They repeat the song as they walk the aisles selling Tootsie Tootsies.)

THE END

Calm Down Mother

by Megan Terry

CALM DOWN MOTHER was first produced (on a double bill with Miss Terry's play *Keep Tightly Closed*) by the Open Theatre in March 1965 at the Sheridan Square Playhouse. It was directed by Richard Gilman. The cast alternated roles throughout the play, beginning as follows:

WOMAN ONE————————————————Sharon Gans
WOMAN THREE————————————————Isabelle Blau
WOMAN TWO————————————————Cynthia Harris

MEGAN TERRY *was born in Seattle, Washington, in 1932. She studied at the University of Washington, the University of Alberta, and the Banff School of Fine Arts. She worked in theatre at the Seattle Repertory Playhouse and the Cornish School. Miss Terry has been a member of the Open Theatre since its inception; she is director of the playwrights' workshop, which meets all day every Saturday. The Open Theatre has produced six of her plays:* Eat at Joe's, Calm Down Mother, Keep Tightly Closed in a Cool Dry Place, Magic Realists, The Gloaming, Oh My Darling, *and* Viet Rock. *She has received a Stanley Drama Award and a grant from the Office for Advanced Drama Research of the University of Minnesota. Her play* Ex-Miss Copper Queen on a Set of Pills *was presented by the Albee-Barr-Playwrights' Unit; other plays have been produced in Seattle and by the Firehouse Theatre in Minneapolis.*

Calm Down Mother
a transformation for three women
by Megan Terry

SCENE

(An open stage. Four chairs are in view. Lights dim up during following speech on tape. Three WOMEN *are clustered together to suggest a plant form.)*

WOMAN'S VOICE

(To be read with the attitude of an amused gentlewoman)
Three one-celled creatures float with currents under the sea. They are propelled at different rates of speed depending upon which current surrounds them. From time to time they reach a byway in the current and float aimlessly. They engulf food whenever they can. When the current changes they are swept into one water force. They come near the shore: the waves push them against the sand: they fall back. Again they are swept up the beach, and again the water pulls them back. Before the next wave hits, they are swept into a small whirlpool where they join together and again are swept up the beach. This time they are not swept back, but take root: one of the first plants to come out of the sea.

A tornado uproots and splits the plant. Two parts fall away. One stretches toward the sun.
(The middle WOMAN *walks toward the audience and smiles at them in joyous wonder.)*

WOMAN ONE

I'm Margaret Fuller. I know I am because . . . "From the time I could speak and go alone, my father addressed me not as a plaything, but as a living mind." I am Margaret Fuller. I am Margaret Fuller and I accept the universe!

TWO WOMEN

(Assuming superior postures)

You had better. You had better. Carlyle said that you had better. You had better. You had better. You bet your butter, Carlyle said that you had better.

WOMAN ONE

I accept. I accept, not as a furry animal plaything, but as a mind, as a living loving blinding mind. My father said . . .

TWO WOMEN

If you know what's good for you, you had better. Better grab that universe, little daughter. Grab it while you can. You had better, you had better. You had better grab it before you melt.

(A brief freeze. Then WOMAN ONE *moves to a store counter. She becomes* SOPHIE. WOMAN THREE *becomes* ESTHER. WOMAN TWO *is a nineteen-year-old* GIRL. *Scene is a delicatessen in Brooklyn.)*

GIRL

(Entering store)

Six packa Ballantine Ale, please.

SOPHIE

(At counter. She stares at GIRL.*)*

Six pack?

(But she doesn't move.)

GIRL

(At first impatient, but then she smiles.)

Make it two six packs.

SOPHIE

Six packs?

ESTHER
She wants ale, Sophie.

SOPHIE
I heard her, Esther.

GIRL
Of Ballantine's. Ballantine Ale.

SOPHIE
Esther, see? Her hair.

ESTHER
So—her hair? What about it? All girls got hairs.

SOPHIE
But it's *her* hair.
   (To the GIRL*)*
Your hair.

GIRL
I'm in a hurry and I'd . . .

SOPHIE
   (Smiling)
It's just like . . . you see, your hair . . . it's just like Mother's
was. Just like it. Same color even.

ESTHER
She ain't got all day. Sophie, you get; I can't reach the
'frigerator.

SOPHIE
   (Reaching toward the GIRL's *hair)*
My hair was like yours . . . but now?
   (She shrugs.)
Surgery.
   (She nods.)
Major operations.

ESTHER

Oy Vey!

SOPHIE

Every time . . . major operations . . . every time I go . . .

ESTHER

Twenty years it was ago!

SOPHIE

Something about the anesthesia. Every time I go under I
come out with less hair.
(She shakes her head and smiles.)
Your hair—it's like hers was. Like mine was, like hers was.
Even more though.

ESTHER

Selfish! Always washing and combing herself. Could never
get ready to go out myself. Some sister!

SOPHIE

She had something to be proud of. She used to say that boys
waited up to eight hours just to take her out.

GIRL

Uh, I'd really like those two six packs of Ballantine's.

SOPHIE

(Moving to GIRL*)*
I know. I got them for you nearly. Let me just touch your
hair. It's so like . . . Something about the anesthetic made
mine go and get straight. See, feel me.

GIRL

Couldn't they uh make tests . . . allergies . . . you should
have tested . . . well you know you may a been allergic to
whatever they knocked you out with . . . Your hair fell out
fer God's sake. It's important to a girl for God's sake. Her
hair. You know what I mean.

SOPHIE
(Nodding sadly)
Well they're interested in pulling you . . . Yes, sure they want to bring you through. Open heart surgery ain't the simplest thing in the world.

ESTHER
(In union with SOPHIE *on last line)*
Open heart surgery ain't the simplest thing in the world.

SOPHIE
But your hair! My mother's hair went in points from here. One point right here and then back and so wavy. Wavy here and here and here. And then it came to a little point in the back. I used to comb it for her when she took her bath. Here, give me the comb, let me do it for you. That's right. Oh Esther you should feel this, so like Momma's. And her skin like milk. And her skin . . . you should . . .

ESTHER
(Talking to God)
Her skin wasn't so hot. My skin's the same. So what's so wrong with my skin? Only sixty years older that's only . . .

SOPHIE
Her skin . . . and then I'd wash her back.
*(*ESTHER *and* GIRL *begin a mournful hum that builds to a lament by the end of the speech.)*
I had skin like her, too, till the blood pressure . . . And then I'd wash her back. And . . . I did. I did it for the last time. Her skin and her hair. I'll never forget the last time, before they put her in her silk . . . before they laid her out you know . . . and everyone came from all over the neighborhood . . . her hair . . . wavy like yours . . . points . . . from here . . . to . . .
(When SOPHIE *joins the lament, the three women are stroking and combing each other's hair. The* GIRL *goes with the*

grief until it arrives at fever pitch—then she feels suffocated and flings the other two women away.)

WOMAN TWO
(To audience)

I want to get to the point in my life where the anger that people send me, the disapproval they show me, the criticism they yell at me can be absorbed by me and sent right on through me into the ground all the way down to China and out the other side.

(She pins her hair back up.)

I can't stand going into these tailspins. I hate the discomfort of it.

(She walks back and leans against WOMAN THREE. *As she walks she throws her feeling to* WOMAN ONE.)*

WOMAN ONE
(During this speech the other women rub their hands together and hiss.)

I want to hit.

(She doubles her fist.)

I want to hit!

(She brings her fist up and shows it to audience.)

I want to hit! I WANT TO HIT!

(She paces back and forth slamming her fist into the other open palm.)

Hit, hit, hit, hit, hit, hit! Bang, Screw! Screw this hitting. All this side of me is aching to hit. It's like a stroke. My left side has nothing more to say.

(She strokes the right side of her head. WOMEN TWO *and* THREE *freeze.)*

This whole part of this side of my head is one red rage and it all adds up to—HIT! I can't sleep any more. When I'm out with people, I have to sit on this hand. I'm so afraid I'll hit someone.

(Her hitting hand comes up across her chest, arcs under her throat and she opens her mouth as her hand and fingers splay open toward the audience. WOMEN TWO *and* THREE *duplicate her gesture. There is a short freeze.)*

WOMAN THREE

(Steps toward audience)

Talk ... Talk ... talk ... lay bare every part of your limited life. Maybe you could force your life to grow into lives. Facts. Add up all the desperate facts, pitiful few facts as they are—add them all up to enter on the human record, short as it is. Keep writing. Maybe if I keep talking and writing, listing all the facts of my life, I won't seem so small, at least not so small to me. When I get scared I can pick up all the lists—all the long lists of the facts of my life and read them out loud to myself, and maybe then I won't feel so crippled, so unconnected—at least not to myself ... A lot of people must start writing with the absurd conviction they are talking to or will contact someone. SOMEONE! SOMEONE! SOMEONE!

WOMEN ONE AND TWO

(Laugh operatically and menace WOMAN THREE, *and beat her down to the floor. Where she lies prone during the next scene.* WOMEN ONE *and* TWO *jump up and down, landing flat, making loud thumping noises. Suddenly they change into New Yorkers in a charming flat.)*

NANCY

(A hearty Oklahoma accent. She's had about ten drinks. Pacing with relish)

So this is your new apartment.

(Her eyes try to glow.)

Why it's very ... it's really very charming. It really is. Downright Greenwich Village, the clean West Side, that is.

(She throws down a heavy leather bag and continues her inspection tour of the small apartment.)

Look at this table. It's perfect.

(If the actress can play this with the gusto of a robust outdoor woman it would be best. However, it's also possible for her to play the entire scene in a semi-catatonic state gripping the back of a chair.)

SALLY

Authentic Goodwill—stripped down by human hands.

(She gets glasses, little snacks)

NANCY

Has he bothered you since? Did you have to get out a restraining order? How do you feel?

(She throws her arms around SALLY and smiles.)

SALLY

Relieved. He hasn't come near since the suit was filed.

NANCY

Good, good, I was worried. You're so soft. I was afraid you'd take him back.

SALLY

I'd rather live with King Farouk and three Bengal tigers.

NANCY

You'd be happier with the tigers. This place is damn cute.

(She winks broadly at SALLY.)

Hey, here we go, ducks.

(She brings a bottle out of her giant bag.)

Scotch. Housewarming! I should have brought champagne to break over your head. Don't get into any more impossible marriages for a few weeks. I need a rest.

SALLY

You old party gal!

(Pouring the drinks)

It's just great to see you, Nan. It's been too too long.

NANCY

It doesn't matter . . . I'm back on the scene now. Back to stay. I hope there'll be enough scenes . . . to make . . . too bad we got you straightened out so fast.
(Reaching for her hand, she says grimly)
Sal, I'm going to fall apart.

SALLY

(Laughing)
Hey, Nan, don't talk like that. Hey, Stella Dallas—snap to!

NANCY

Yeah, yeah, Lolly baby—old Stell will come through—old bulwark of the family. The fight settler. Held Sister together through divorce. Settled Granddaddy's estate. Got Jorgensen into State Assembly. Oh, Christ, Sal . . . hold on to me . . . I can't any more . . .
(She downs her drink.)

SALLY

Nancy, what . . . what is it? What can I do?

NANCY

I wish someone could do . . . what? But there's nothing. I've done everything possible. Brought her up to Harkness Pavilion . . . Every expert in the East. Then last night . . . got the corroborative diagnosis.

SALLY

Nancy, Nan . . . for you . . . ?

NANCY

Mother . . . it's "terminal bone cancer." Sal, it's not fair. It is *not* fair. She's such a fighter. My God, she began a whole new career when Dad retired to his bottle of booze. No training, only her guts . . . good taste. Do you know she knows as much about fashion as I do? She always knew. She knew how to see. She *knows* how to see. So what happens, does this snap him back to reality? No. She's dying, so Dad fakes a heart attack. I've been on the phone with Sister all night. Who's in the hospital. Who's getting all the attention? He is!

SALLY

But Nan, maybe he really . . . needs . . .

NANCY

Such a fighter. Like me. No, I'm like her. Give me a light, will you . . . I can't make these matches work. Thanks, I'm fond of you, you know that?

SALLY

Nan, I never could have made it through the breakup without you.

NANCY

Men, you can't live with them and all that jazz. . . .

SALLY

Nancy, how long?

NANCY

Six months, 180 days. I can't accept it.

SALLY

When are you leaving for Tulsa?

NANCY

I was going to take the next plane, but the doctor talked me out of it. You see, if I suddenly appear—you see—she'll think it's the end. If the children all swoop home and stand around the bed, it means, in her mind, she only has hours left. . . . I can't go to her until it really *is* the end. Oh God, Sal, how am I going to stand it? I'll be dying for her every day, every goddamned day from now till . . . till . . .

(SALLY *and* NANCY *embrace and freeze.*)

WOMAN THREE

(Comes up from her floor bed and moves downstage with ex-uberant motion. Kneels and speaks to audience)

> Once upon a green time . . .
> Once upon a green time . . .
> My girlhood was still all flowers
> > all flowers
> > all flowers . . .

(She freezes for an instant, then rises. She walks upstage and turns her back on the other two. WOMEN ONE and TWO sit in two chairs facing audience. They are two chairs in a nursing home.)

MRS. TWEED

Ah, yes, Mrs. Watermellon, and the days go by and the days go by and the days go by and the days go by, and by and by the days go by. My God, how the days go by!

MRS. WATERMELLON

From where I sit . . . I have to agree with you. But they don't go fast enough by, Mrs. Tweed, not by a half sight, not by a full sight. The world is waiting for the sunrise, and I'm the only one who knows where it begins.

MRS. TWEED

Why do you keep it a secret?

MRS. WATERMELLON

No secret. I've told everyone. I've told and told and told everyone.

MRS. TWEED

Where *does* it begin then?

MRS. WATERMELLON

(Clasping her breast)

Here, right here, right here it starts. From the old ticker it starts and pumps and pumps around and thumps around,

267

coagulates in my belly and once a month bursts out onto the ground . . . but all the color's gone . . . all but one . . . all but one . . .

MRS. TWEED

You shouldn't think of such things. Woman a' yore age.

MRS. WATERMELLON

You're so much! You three-minute egg! You runny, puny, twelve-weeks-old, three-minute egg. You're underdone and overripe. What do you know? You only learned to speak when you got mad enough. I'm going to sleep. I'd as soon live in the mud with the turtles as have to converse with the likes of you.

MRS. TWEED

I'm going to call your mother. I'll fly her here on a plane and have her commit you. I'm going to phone your son. I'm going to fly him here on a plane and have you committed. I am. I will. You'll be committed.

MRS. WATERMELLON

Dry up, you old fart. I already am.

NURSE
(Entering with tray)
Time for cream of wheat.
(She smiles as she says this, but her voice is flat and mechanical.)
Time for your creamy wheat. Time for your wheat. Your cream's all gone. Time for the heap the wheat's all dry. Sit up like good wrinkled girls and dribble it down your chins. Time for your cream of wheat, the sugar's all gone.

MRS. WATERMELLON

I'm tired of being a middleman for that pap. Flush it down the nearest john!

NURSE

I'll eat it myself. I'll eat it all up.

MRS. TWEED

(Standing and whirling to face NURSE.*)*

It's worms. Look at her eat the pail of wiggly worms.

MRS. WATERMELLON

(Joining TWEED.*)*

You got it all wrong, you three-eyed egg. That's the worm,
and she's eating herself.

(The NURSE *tries to get through them but the* TWO WOMEN
*become a subway door. They open and close and chant the
while.)*

TWO WOMEN

Please keep your hands off the doors.
Please keep your hands off the doors.
Please keep your hands off the doors.
Please keep your hands off the doors.
Please keep your hands off the doors.
Please keep your hands off the doors.
Please keep your hands off the doors.
Please keep your hands off the doors.
Please keep your hands off the doors.
Please keep your hands off the doors.
Please keep your hands off the doors.

(One WOMAN *breaks through—goes to the chairs and sits.
They are now call-girls in a lush apartment. Each is dressing
and applying make-up.)*

MOMO

What are you smirking for. You walk around here like you
had the biggest prick in the world.

FELICIA

And you're jealous.

MOMO

I do all right.

FELICIA

Don't open your yap if you can't back it up.

MOMO

I could back it up to you.

FELICIA

Not any more you couldn't. I could take anyone away from you.

INEZ

Shut up, you two. We'll never be ready for the first party.

MOMO

Well make her get off my back.

FELICIA

With spikes.

MOMO

She turns on me. Why you get so nervous whenever we have to ball a gang? It isn't as if you never did it before.

FELICIA

I'll stick holes in your diaphragm. Let me see in the mirror.

INEZ

Felicia, come over here. There's plenty of room.

FELICIA

I can't see in that mirror. The light's no good.

MOMO

You can't see, period. You've got your mascara half way down your navel.

FELICIA

Bugger off, you—or I'll put alum on your tits.

270

INEZ

Dry up, Felicia! We've got to get ready for work.

FELICIA

Make her stop.

INEZ

I'm going to call Ricky. I'm gonna throw you both out. She can't saddle me with inexperienced bums!

MOMO AND FELICIA

Who's inexperienced?

INEZ

You are!

MOMO AND FELICIA

We've turned more tricks in the last year than . . .

INEZ

Balls! You don't know how to handle yourselves. You don't know how to even get ready to work. What you burning up all your good working energy yapping at each other? You don't stop fighting, I'll boil both you bitches in oil and circumcise your snatches!

FELICIA

Calm down, mother. I can keep Momo in line by telling Ricky . . .

MOMO

You can't tell Ricky any . . .

FELICIA

(Pulls out a roll of bills)

Oh no? What's this? Looks like money—looks like you've been stashing your tips in the bathtub water spout.

MOMO

I never . . .

FELICIA

You forgot to clean out your hiding place last night, but I didn't.

MOMO

You took it . . . you crosseyed sonofa——

INEZ

(Coming between them and grabbing money)

I'll take that. Ricky gets that. What's the matter with you, Momo? Girls have drowned in acid for less than that. You want to ruin your nest?

MOMO

It wasn't a regular lay, it was a piece of cake. He just wanted to look at me. All I had to do was take off my clothes and climb the furniture and spread my fur . . . it wasn't work. I'm saving up for . . .

INEZ

Saving up for what?

MOMO

My vacation. I never been south of Jersey.

INEZ

If Ricky ever found out, we'd all get bumped. I'm responsible for us. It takes us five nights to knock down the rent of this place, we work another week to pay off the fuzz, that leaves two weeks to split with Ricky and the three of us. What if we had to pay income tax, too? For Christ's sakes we couldn't afford to put out!

MOMO

Don't tell Ricky, for God's sake don't tell . . .

INEZ

I'll give you one more chance. One. You get that? One. One don't mean two! All right? All right.

FELICIA

Move it. I need this mirror to finish my make-up. I'm near-sighted and you shouldn't hold it against me.

MOMO

I wouldn't hold anything against . . .

INEZ

That's enough, that's *enough*!

MOMO

I'm sick of you two ganging up on me!

INEZ

I think you'll turn into a real swinger, kid, but you got a lot to learn. You're still on probation.

MOMO

All right. I'm sorry. What should I do—tear out my ovaries?

INEZ

Keep your nose clean, and sweeten that sour mouth. The both of yez!

FELICIA

(Throws herself in INEZ's *arms)*

Oh, Momma baby, mommie, mommie. We won't fight. We won't do it any more. We didn't mean to get you mad.

INEZ

I should blister you till you couldn't sit down.

FELICIA

(Turns her bottom up for spanking)

Do it. We're bad. Bad, bad girls.

MOMO

(Nearly on her knees—she does the same.)

Bad, bad, bad, we should have a spanking.

INEZ

Stop pawing me. Stop that now. You're spoiling my make-up.

(They are in physical contact at this moment. Two are touching, one resisting. They freeze and—

The WOMEN *form a triangle and throw sentences to each other. The one who receives repeats before she sends on the next new sentence.)*

WOMAN ONE

Have confidence.

WOMAN TWO

Have confidence. You've been found.

WOMAN THREE

You've been found. Have confidence.

WOMAN ONE

Have confidence. You've been found.

WOMAN TWO

You've been found. Have confidence.

WOMAN THREE

Have confidence.

TOGETHER

You've been found!

(They break the formal attitude and tease and walk about. Asking it as a question "You've been found? I've been found. Oh, you've been found? No, I've been found." They assume positions of co-operative dish washing at a tenement sink. SUE *who puts dishes away tries to read a magazine at the same time.)*

SUE

(Slapping down the magazine.)

All this birth control jazz. Who're they kidding? Being mad

if you don't let a baby happen? That old dame Mother Nature does it every month—and look, Ma, no rubber!

SAK

What're you talking about, no rubber?

SUE

No rubber, stupid. Tampax!

SAK

Moron, that's for your period.

SUE

And it puts a period to the egg, too, don't it, stupid?

MA

I want you girls should stop arguing and fighting all the time.

SUE

She's too stupid to argue and fight with me.

MA

The Bible says you shouldn't cast thy seed upon the ground.

SAK

That applies to the fellas, Ma.

SUE

You see, you see how dumb you are? What you think grows up in your belly every month—cotton candy?

SAK

Make her stop.

MA

You should stop, Sue.
(MA *and* SAK *sit on chairs side by side.*)

SUE

I never started it, Ma. That old boy you fall down on your

knees and talk to every night—he started it. And he started it here.

(She slaps her belly.)

Guys got seeds and girls got seeds, and if that old old old garden planter planted all the damn seeds in the first place, he fixed it so's they wouldn't all grow. They fall on the ground of their own accord, so then? So then, who the hell, then, then who the holy hell are all these priests and magazine writers to say it's wrong? Who the hell are all these guys on platforms to say you can't take pills, you can't use rubbers, down with vaseline, out with diaphragms, who the hell then are they? For God's sake. They're all preventing life!

SAK

Make her stop talking like that, Ma. It's just you, Sue, you feeling guilty. You, 'cause you're taking them pills, and you know you shouldn't ought.

SUE

Get off my back and get some brains, for God's sake. Listen to me. If you can focus your dirty ears. I'm twenty years old, right?

SAK

Twenty and three months.

SUE

Je-sus!

SAK

Well you are.

SUE

Christ. I'm twenty, see, and I'm good till I'm fifty, see. Judging from Ma.

MA

Sue!

SUE

For God's sake, Ma. You're a female ain't you? You didn't
have your period now for three years, right?

(MA *counts on her fingers and nods.*)

So I figure I'm good fer as long as you, so—that makes
thirty years still, see?

SAK

All you think about is one thing, all you think about is . . .

SUE

All I'm trying to prove to you is a proven scientific fact,
that is all I'm trying to do to you.

SAK

You're disseminating, that's what you're doing.

SUE

In your eye! Oh, God. I can't believe you're my sister. Ma,
tell me you chose, and only her out of thousands of up-
turned faces at the orphanage. Please, please?

MA

Stop it, the both of you.

SUE

Well, I didn't. See, I got enough eggs in me for thirty years,
see. That's one a month for thirty years. Twelve times
thirty is—360 eggs. Three hundred and sixty possibilities.
Three hundred and sixty babies could be born out of my
womb. So, if I don't produce each and every one of them,
which is a mathematical impossibility, should I go to hell
for that? So what should I do—pray and moan on beans?
So what should I do, catch eggs and save them in a test tube
for when after the BOMB comes? And I'm only one bearer
of the eggs. You sitting on yours, you're nineteen. You got
a whole year's eggs on me still. So if God sees fit to flush

277

them down the pipe every month if they don't meet up with an electric male shock, then who the hell are these priests and all to scream about pills and controls? Tell me that! Who the hell are they? They want to save my eggs till they can get around to making them into babies, they can line up and screw the test tubes. Yeah! That's a sight. They're welcome. But they can't shoot twins into my test tubes. And you two! You sit there in the church every Sunday, kneeling and mumbling and believing all that crap that those men tell you, and they don't even know what the hell they are talking about. And I'll bet you don't know what I'm talking about. Because I'm the only one in this whole carton of eggs what's got any brains. And I'm taking my pills and I ain't kneeling on any beans or babies' brains to make up for it.

(The three resume dish washing.)

SAK

You'll burn in the fire for what you just said. . . .

SUE

They'll make me a saint! A thousand years from now they'll award me a medal for not contributing to the population!

SAK

All the candles in the world lit like the stars couldn't get you into Purgatory even.

SUE

Good, then I won't have to be with you.

SAK

You know why she's talking that way, Ma. You know what she's been doing and why she's taking them pills? Where's her husband, Ma? Where's the guy? When's the marriage, Ma? Look at her. She never comes home till four in the morning, Ma. And me, I never stay out past ten.

278

SUE

Cause nobody asks you that's why.

MA

Pack your things.

SUE

Ah, Ma.

MA

You're no daughter of mine. You pack your things!

SUE

I was only trying to prove . . .

MA

You proved what you are to me all right . . . you pack your things.

SUE

But Ma?

MA

Pack your things.

SUE

I'm proving.

MA

Pack . . . you!

SUE

Ma! I been born out of my time. Or you never left yours. That's right—three hundred years old that's what you are. You two escapees from Shangri-la. You wrinkle brains, you vegetables, you empty bottles of holy water. I'll go, all right! I don't need any bags. I got everything I need right here in my belly. I got everything I need for the next thirty years, and how!

(The three stand together and smile at the audience. They then speak to it slowly, sweetly, like amused gentlewomen.)

279

TOGETHER
(They place their hands on bellies.)
Our bellies

WOMAN TWO
(On sides)
Our bodies

TOGETHER
(Back on bellies)
Our bellies

TOGETHER
(On bellies)
Our bellies

WOMAN THREE
(On sides)
Our bodies

TOGETHER
(On bellies)
Our bellies

WOMAN ONE
(On breasts)
Our funnies

TOGETHER
(Bellies)
Our bellies

WOMAN TWO
(Sides)
Bodies

WOMAN ONE
(Bellies)
Our eggies

WOMAN THREE
(Bellies)
Our eggies

WOMAN TWO
(Bellies)
The eggies in our beggies

WOMAN ONE
(Sides)
Are enough

WOMAN TWO
(Sides)
Are enough.

WOMAN THREE
(Sides)
Are enough

TOGETHER
(Turn their backs on audience)
ARE THEY?

CURTAIN

ILLUSTRATIONS

Taylor Mead and Veronica Castang in THE GENERAL RETURNS FROM ONE PLACE TO ANOTHER courtesy Michael Harvest

Neil Flanagan in THE MADNESS OF LADY BRIGHT courtesy Conrad Ward

Kevin O'Connor in CHICAGO courtesy Robert J. Margouleff

Gil Henderson and Ray Girardin in THE GREAT AMERICAN DESERT courtesy Judson Poets' Theatre

BALLS courtesy Amy

The Motel-Keeper Doll in AMERICA HURRAH courtesy Phill Niblock

James Barbosa, Barbara Vann, and Paul Boesing in THE SUCCESSFUL LIFE OF 3 courtesy Phill Niblock

Sharon Gans, Cynthia Harris, and Isabelle Blau in CALM DOWN MOTHER courtesy Phill Niblock

812.08 Orzel, Nick ,ed.
0 Eight plays from
off-off Broadway.

Wilmington Public Library
Wilmington, N. C.

2/67

RULES

1. ~~Books marked 7 days may be kept one week. Books marked 14 days, two weeks. The latter may be renewed, if more than 6 months old.~~

2. ~~A fine of two cents a day will be charged on each book which is not returned according to the above rule.~~ No book will be issued to any person having a fine of 25 cents or over.

3. A charge of ten cents will be made for mutilated plastic jackets. All injuries books beyond reasonable wear and all losses shall be made good to the satisfaction of the Librarian.

4. Each borrower is held responsible for all books drawn on his card and for all fines acing on the same.